STAYING POWER

STAYING POWER

*WHY PEOPLE LEAVE THE
CHURCH OVER CHANGE
(AND WHAT YOU CAN DO ABOUT IT!)*

BOB WHITESEL

Abingdon Press/Nashville

STAYING POWER
WHY PEOPLE LEAVE THE CHURCH OVER CHANGE
(AND WHAT YOU CAN DO ABOUT IT!)

Library of Congress Cataloging-in-Publication Data

Whitesel, Bob.
  Staying power : why people leave the church over change (and what you can do about it!) / Bob Whitesel.
    p. cm.
  ISBN 0-687-06680-8 (pbk. : alk. paper)
  1. Church growth. I. Title.

BV652.25.W495 2003
254'.5—dc21   2002155981

03 04 05 06 07 08 09 10 11 12—10 9 8 7 6 5 4 3 2 1

MANUFACTURED IN THE UNITED STATES OF AMERICA

CONTENTS

Preface 7

Acknowledgments 11

CHAPTER ONE
A New Understanding of an Old Problem 13

CHAPTER TWO
A Quickstart Guide: How to Use This Book 18

PART ONE: HOW EXITS DESTROY CHURCHES

CHAPTER THREE
The Pain (and Gain) of Exits 33

CHAPTER FOUR
A Tale of One Church in Two Parts 41

PART TWO: HOW PEOPLE EXIT A CHURCH IN SIX STAGES

CHAPTER FIVE
Stage 1: Relative Harmony 53

CHAPTER SIX
Stage 2: When New Ideas Are Introduced 67

CHAPTER SEVEN
Stage 3: Change 76

CHAPTER EIGHT
Stage 4: Resistance 94

CHAPTER NINE
Stage 5 (On Route A): Intense Conflict 109

CHAPTER TEN
Stage 5 (On Route B): Dissonant Harmony 127

CHAPTER ELEVEN
Stage 6: Group Exit or Retention? 148

CHAPTER TWELVE
Two Actions and an Attitude That Can Keep Your Change
Proponents (and Your Status Quo Too!) 169

Appendix A: How Group Exit Occurs (and Why) 178

Appendix B: A Recap of Our *Exit Antidotes* 183

Notes 190

PREFACE

Enthusiasm can only be aroused by two things:
First, an ideal which takes the imagination by storm,
and second, a definite intelligible plan for carrying
that ideal into practice.
—*Arnold Toynbee, historian*[1]

An Ideal That Takes the Imagination by Storm

One of the most baffling questions facing church leaders today is why people leave the church over change and what can be done about it.

Most church leaders are all too familiar with a scenario where certain church attendees suggest change that they believe will enhance a church's ministry. Initially, other congregants may appear receptive and usually inaugural changes will be adopted. But all too often disagreements over the degree or rapidity of change soon polarize factions within the church.

Mismanaging change can be devastating. Often, a group of people will leave the church. Such exits are especially heart wrenching because they sever relationships, damage congregational self-esteem, and rob a church of its essential constituents.

In this book the reader will learn that change and the tensions that accompany it are not only inevitable but also *survivable*. The reader will also discover that change does not have to result in group exit. This vital ideal can take the imagination of church leaders by storm. Still, an intelligible plan is required.

7

An Intelligible Plan for Carrying That Ideal into Practice

In search of this plan, I began to research the change process and why most churches fail at this effort. I noticed that, once a church started to initiate change, it would soon experience polarization between those who wanted the change and those who felt the change went too far or was not warranted. I watched as churches, especially churches under 200 in attendance, were torn apart and even died because of a mismanaged change process. With this in mind, I began a thorough and meticulous quest to understand and describe the processes that bring about change in a constructive manner.

I discovered that there is a straightforward and precise six-stage process that churches undergo when implementing change, and by simply altering two parts of this process, change can take place without an accompanying group exit. This book is an explanation of that strategic process:

- There is a six-stage process that churches undergo when trying to implement change.
- There are five triggers that push a church out of one stage and into the next.
- Groups in the church will naturally polarize over change, but there are actions a church can employ to prevent alienation.
- If the change process is not managed properly, groups of people will leave a church.
- By adjusting two of the five triggers group retention can result instead of group exit.

Learning Aids Included in This Book

To grasp the change process, I have developed five learning aids:

1. "Exit Antidotes" that encapsulate the basic lessons of each chapter.

2. "Questions for Group Study" at the end of most chapters. They are intended to help readers pinpoint exactly where they are in the change process.
3. Footnotes at the end of each chapter to give the reader access to the original research sources.
4. A graphic representation of the change process as a series of stages and triggering events.
5. A "Quickstart Guide" in chapter 2. This diagnostic guide can help a church enmeshed in the change process quickly discover the stage it is undergoing and which chapters in this book would be most applicable. If you are embroiled or headed toward conflict over change, go directly to chapter 2.

Putting a Strategy into Practical Terms

With a wedding of personal field experience, academic research, and client support, I began my quest to put this information into the hands of the average layperson, denominational executive, and pastor. This book is the culmination of that quest.

Dr. Bob Whitesel
Creative Church Consulting Intl.
Winona Lake, IN 46590-0788
www.c3intl.org

ACKNOWLEDGMENTS

In my life, the Lord seems to be especially adroit at accomplishing his will through four avenues: my parents, my professors, my partner, and my progeny.

My parents, Gerald and Fern Whitesel, tirelessly answered hours of my adolescent questionings about God, eternity, and Jesus Christ. Their convincing and unwearied exposition forever consigned an understanding of God's love and sacrifice to my heart.

My professors, George E. Ladd, C. Peter Wagner, and Eddie Gibbs, added the requisite intellectual knowledge. They introduced me to the writings of Emil Brunner, who demonstrated that the church was not just a spiritual entity, but also an organization that must be managed.[1] Colleagues in the field of management—Kent Miller, Roger Finke, Bruno Dyck, David Wright, Mark Smith, Brad Grubb, and Kevin Dougherty along with church-growth thinkers such as Kent Hunter, Elmer Towns, Gary McIntosh, Chip Arn, and George Hunter—were indispensable.

The final touch was administered by my wife, Rebecca, and our amazing offspring. Through her gentle nudgings, my wife became one of the Holy Spirit's primary avenues into my life. And, my children, Breanna, Kelly, Carrie, and Ashley, taught me how to live the Christian life to the fullest, as I witnessed their youthful spirituality overflow into church, friendships, and ministry.

All of these influences instilled in me a love for the church and a desire to see her vibrant, effervescent, and growing. To them, and my Lord Jesus, I dedicate this volume.

CHAPTER 1

A New Understanding of an Old Problem

*"We must continue to recognize that
humanity is a mosaic."*
—Donald R. McGavran[1]

Discovering a Plan for Harmonious Change

In this book, I am exploring how churches attempt to bring about change, but usually only divide the congregation into competing camps with divergent views. I have labeled these competing camps the "change proponents" and the "status quo."

In my work as a church growth consultant for more than a decade, I have witnessed the outcome of the change process in varied scenarios. Regrettably, the end result of most attempts at change is polarization and the eventual exit of a group of church attendees, most often those who wanted change.[2] Thus the title *Staying Power* seemed an appropriate designation for a book that investigates a strategy that fosters staying power.

Moving from a Melting Pot Image to a Stew Pot Image

Some may question if it is always better for change proponents and the status quo to remain together in the same church. I have found that if a church retains both groups, it will usually be healthier and more resilient due to a broader base of diverse constituents.

C. Peter Wagner, in his look at why groups join churches, suggests that the "melting pot" analogy, popular when describing America, may be an inappropriate designation for churches. The melting pot analogy implies that the Native Americans and immigrants who populate North America are being slowly melted into a new culture through the forces of assimilation. But Wagner believes that a "stew pot" is a better analogy for a church. He reasons that in a stew pot, "each ingredient adds its characteristic flavor to the every other ingredient, but all maintain their own identities and integrity. . . . It is a new product, colorful and flavorful to a degree that would have been impossible for any of the ingredients taken alone."[3] Thus, Wagner paints a valuable image of the church as an amalgamation of people happily and heartily coexisting.

Donald McGavran, pioneer of church growth, preferred the image of a mosaic, stating that "church growth ardently maintains that we must continue to recognize that humanity is a mosaic. . . . The growth of the church will not meld green, white, black, yellow, purple, and red pieces of the mosaic into one dark gray piece."[4] McGavran reminds us that the church is not a drab unappealing mixture. It is a rich and multihued blend of personalities and preferences.

Into this mix must come tools for managing the tensions that arise when ingredients of this stew pot come into conflict. Though the potentials for conflict are manifold, this book will address how to bring about harmony among two of the church's primary ingredients: change proponents and the status quo.

The Need for a Strategic Map of the Change Process

With these observations in mind, I began to map out how the change process could be managed so that it retained both change proponents and the status quo. Over nearly a decade, I sketched out a rough graph of the basic stages. When my clients employed this process, I happily discovered that change proponents could be retained in a congregation.

But I needed more insight. The process worked but I did not have a universal map in my mind. Then, as I sat down one day with a colleague, the pieces fell into place.

Kent Miller is a professor of strategic management at the Krannert School of Management at Purdue University. But when Kent speaks of the church, his eyes flash with sparks of concern and apprehension. Kent is a pioneer in the field of strategic church management. Scouring academic journals, querying colleagues, researching church management, and accumulating one of the largest files I have seen on church research, Kent is a treasure trove of insight.

In one conversation, I casually lamented how a mismanaged change process often resulted in groups leaving the church. I told him that I had a developing understanding of the process, but not a clear-cut and universal strategy that could be verified by research.

"I have what you want," replied Kent. "Are you familiar with Dyck and Starke? They have been researching what you are after." Pulling an article in the *Administrative Science Quarterly* from his desk, Kent handed me the missing ingredients to the process I had so diligently tried to codify.

Eureka! Someone Has Discovered the Steps and Triggers of Exit Behavior

Bruno Dyck and Frederick Starke are researchers in the Department of Business Administration at the University of Manitoba, and they had put together the framework for how the change process works.[5] Here, hidden among the pages of a scholarly journal and cloaked in the precise, yet intimidating, language of academia, was the helpful prescription for a problem that besets so many pastors and church leaders—*how do you keep people from leaving the church over change?*

I read with excitement as Dyck and Starke described the change process as a series of stages, accompanied by triggering events that pushed the church out of one stage and into the next. While I had comprehended the stages, the universality of the triggering events was a revelation.

In addition, Dyck and Starke discovered that simply changing two of the triggering events could prevent group exit and implement change successfully. Those two triggers are . . .

Ah, but I am getting ahead of my story. To accurately grasp the process requires that some groundwork be laid. Therefore, in the following chapters, we will investigate each of the stages (and triggers) that can lead to group exit or retention.

Field Research: Comparing Process to Practice

I spent the next year and a half updating my model of the change process and applying the results to my clients. This afforded me the opportunity to study the group retention process in churches of all sizes and across a broad spectrum of denominational affiliations.

I found the six steps and five triggers held up in almost all scenarios. With the gracious support of Dyck, Starke, and Miller, I undertook the task of penning a book that would clearly outline this process for the church leader.

To increase the book's readability, I decided to include real-life stories of churches that have overcome or succumbed to the change process. Here, I encountered a moderate degree of resistance from churches I intended to cite. Many clients were hesitant to allow their church's misfortune with the change process to be publicly broadcast.

As a result, my clients recommended an option I have adopted in this book. They suggested I use pseudonyms and interweave several stories to illustrate the point under consideration. Though I felt this could slightly undermine the veracity of my illustrations, I acquiesced out of respect for my clients.

The Next Step

Our journey through the change process begins with a "Quickstart Guide" in chapter 2, which allows the reader to quickly consult those portions of the book that pertain to the stage their church is undergoing.

CHAPTER 2

A Quickstart Guide: How to Use This Book

Do what you can, with what you have, where you are.
—Theodore Roosevelt [1]

What to Do If You Are Facing a Group Exit

If you are in a congregation that is undergoing an exit of attendees, informally or formally, you may already be experiencing the process outlined in this book. At such junctures, it is important to act quickly if you hope to stem the tide of people leaving the church. Expediency can be especially crucial for churches with fewer than 200 attendees, where group exits can rapidly deplete a significant portion of the talent and treasures of a congregation.

The following is a "Quickstart Guide" which will help you immediately begin the process of diagnosing your situation and locating the appropriate steps you can take to halt an exit of people from your congregation.

The majority of this guide will cover terminology that is important for understanding the highly charged realm of group exits. Then I will describe each of the six stages of the group exit process along with their five triggers. Finally, this Quickstart Guide will conclude with seven questions that can help you quickly grasp which stage you are undergoing, and allow you to skip ahead to the correct chapter that addresses the problem.

New Terminology for an Old Problem

Research on how and why people leave the church has been developed in the rather isolated realm of academia and often seems unintelligible to the average layperson. Some of the academic descriptions, however, are very helpful, and yield a new precision to our understanding of the problem. My goal has been to refine these terms into designations that help preserve the insights gleaned by researchers, while making them easily understood by the church leader.

Here, then, is a list of terms:

"GROUP EXIT"

Group exit is defined as the exit or departure of a group of people from regular participation in the life of a church. This means that the exiting persons disunite with the church either by withdrawing their membership or, more often, by halting their attendance at church activities. Groups can range in size from a small group of eight to twelve people to as large as a group of 175 people (sometimes called a subcongregation).[2]

"ATTENDEES" AND "MEMBERS"

The people leaving the church may not be official members. Many times, group exits consist of "attendees" who have either recently begun attending the church or feel no personal need to officially join the church's membership rolls.

"Members" are congregants who have formally become members of the church.

"INFORMAL" AND "FORMAL" EXITS

Groups can leave a church informally or formally. "Informal exits" take place when attendees slowly trickle out of the church without a formal or structured plan. The defining characteristic of informal exits is that they are not consciously organized.

In the "formal exit," an organized exit of a group will take place. Sometimes, an official or unofficial leader will actually woo these people away as a group. In other circumstances, a nearby church may actively recruit the dissatisfied members. Either way, a formal exit involves organization and structure.

Formal exits can take the form of a church split; a church plant; or moving a Bible study or Sunday school class to a neutral location, or even to another congregation.

THE "MULTI-GENERATIONAL (MULTI-GEN)" CHURCH

Group exits often happen when a church is reaching out to several age groups at once. But, developing into a congregation with several age groups is a healthy strategy as well as important for survival. Congregations that are primarily made up of one generation generally grow old with that age group, and will eventually expire. This aging of the congregation is the number-one killer of churches in America.[3] Developing into a multi-generational or "multi-gen" church is, oftentimes, the best way to save aging churches.

In my earlier book, *A House Divided: Bridging the Generation Gaps in Your Church,* I gave a detailed definition of a multi-generational church.[4] However, for the present discussion, the Multi-Gen church can be thought of as one organization, under one name and one leadership team, that has three or more active and healthy generations peacefully coexisting: Builders, Boomers, Generation X, and Generation Y.

Several strengths of the Multi-Gen church important for the present discussion are:

- *Physical health.* A church that has recruited and mentored younger generations to take the mantle of leadership will not die due to the aging of its long-time members. Youthful leaders will be in place to ensure that the baton is passed to the next generation.

- *Financial health.* The fiscal base of the Multi-Gen church is shared by three generations. Often, the senior generation will live on a fixed income. Generation X will be just starting careers and unable to help significantly. In such cases, the Multi-Gen church allows more prosperous segments of the church, such as those in the fiscal power years of the mid-forties to mid-fifties, to share a greater portion of the financial responsibility.

- *Relational health.* The Multi-Gen church provides an environment where regular interaction between generations—grandparent, parent, and child—can take place.

- *Spiritual health.* The Multi-Gen church produces an atmosphere where religious beliefs can be readily passed down from grandparent to grandchild. Anthropologist Margaret Mead discovered that spiritual beliefs are more easily passed down from grandparent to grandchild than from parent to child.[5] However, because most churches are comprised of one primary generation, this trans-generational communication of sacred beliefs is hindered. The Multi-Gen strategy provides a trans-generational environment that addresses this dilemma.

"BUILDERS," "BOOMERS," "GEN-X," AND "GEN-Y"

An understanding of different generational cultures is one of the most important requisites for church leaders. In my earlier book, I offered an analysis of these generations and what they are looking for in a church, as well as an in-depth look at the different worship styles and ministry approaches that each generation prefers.[6]

For the present discussion, I will give a brief overview of the generations and their age ranges.

Generational Name	Birth Years	How They Got Their Name
The Builders	Born in and before 1945	They "built" the U.S. into a worldwide military and economic power.

The Boomers	1946–1964	Borrowed from Old West parlance where a "boom town" was a town that grew up overnight, the dramatic rise in birth rates after World War II led to this designation.
Generation X	1965–1983	Originally so named because of a perceived penchant for nihilism, pollsters have found they are remarkably religious and not nearly so rebellious as their name implies.[7]
Generation Y or the Millennials	1984–2001	Born after Gen-X but immediately before and during the millennial changeover, they are affected by the rapid rise in technology and the tensions of living in a global community.

"CROSS-GENERATIONAL SURFERS"

Also present within the church are "cross-generational surfers." These are church attendees or members who naturally surf, or cross over, and identify with other age groups. Some may actually dress and behave like an older or younger generation. Others will simply demonstrate an understanding and solidarity with a different generation. Either way, these cross-generational surfers remind us that we cannot gauge a person's generational sympathies simply by knowing their age.

"CHANGE PROPONENTS"

"Change proponents" do exactly what their name says—they promote change. They often see change as a healthy adaptation of the church's ministries into forms that are more in keeping with contemporary culture.

The motivation of true change proponents is not change for change's sake but, rather, to bring about change that will adapt the good news without altering the content. They do not seek to change the message, only the techniques through which the message is shared.[8]

THE "STATUS QUO"

The "status quo" are individuals for whom the existing methods and traditions of the church are so meaningful that they detest the thought of losing them by changing to new methods.

What creates the status quo? Members of the status quo usually have one or more of the following convictions:

• The status quo have been so touched by some program or event in the past that they hate to see it eliminated even though it has ceased to be productive. An example is the church "revival," a period of renewal meetings. Some of the status quo may have had such a positive experience with a revival in the past, that they now steadfastly refuse to see it end, even after it is evident that it is not reaching the unchurched as it once did.

• A majority of the status quo may be older members of a congregation. By the very fact of their long-standing participation in the church, they will have an appreciation for the church's traditional strategies and will want to preserve them. The programs to which they have grown accustomed provide stability in their waning years, as fixed incomes and health problems put insecurity in almost all other areas of their lives. They actively resist changes that will thrust more uncertainty into their lives.

• The status quo is not limited to older members of a congregation. Many younger people may align with the status quo because of a long family history in the church. Such a history usually has increased their appreciation for the traditions embraced by the status quo.

THE "STAGES" OF GROUP EXIT

In this book, we will look at the six stages or phases a church goes through before a group exits. Each of these stages has its own characteristics, and most have their own triggering event.

The six stages of group exit are:

STAGE 1: *Relative Harmony.* The church exists in a general state of concord.

STAGE 2: *Idea Development.* Individuals in the church (who will eventually form a recognizable subgroup) become convinced that the church is in need of change.

STAGE 3: *Change.* The change proponents form a recognizable subgroup within the congregation (they may even have their own name) and implement change.

STAGE 4: *Resistance.* The status quo coalesce into a recognizable subgroup to challenge the changes and to defend their traditions. The change proponents step up their efforts to overcome this resistance to change.

STAGE 5: *Intense Conflict.* Members of both the status quo and the change proponents expect other church attendees to take sides.

STAGE 6: *Group Exit.* The rift between the change proponents and the status quo becomes so deep that one group, usually the change proponents, breaks away and exits the congregation.

"TRIGGER EVENTS"

"Trigger events" are actions or occasions that help push a church out of one stage and into another. There are five triggers in the exit process but two of these events are "negative trigger events" and have significant detrimental outcomes. However, when each of these two "negative trigger events" is replaced with a "positive trigger event," the group exit will usually *not* occur. The two negative events have positive alternatives, a crucial fact that is not usually understood by church leaders. In the following chapters, the reader will see that if Triggers 2 and 4 (the two negative trigger events) are replaced with positive trigger events, then groups will usually remain in the church and bring about change in a harmonious and appropriate manner.

The Six Stages of Group Exit

The Stages of Group Exit When Accompanied by Negative Trigger Events

The interrelationship between the five stages and four triggering events can best be explained by putting them in order. We will first look at how the five stages of group exit occur when accompanied by negative trigger events. Elements that are added to the above list are italicized for emphasis.

STAGE 1: Relative Harmony. The church exists in a general state of concord.

Trigger 1: *Conflicting Ideas Event. Some members attend a seminar or other idea-generating event where they get excited about new ideas that conflict with the church's customary way of operating.*

STAGE 2: Idea Development. Individuals become convinced that the church is in need of change.

Trigger 2: *Negative Legitimizing Event. The change propo-nents' new ideas are inadvertently substantiated or blessed. This may happen when a pastor or influential layperson publicly and vocally supports the new idea.*

STAGE 3: Change. The change proponents form a subgroup and implement change.

Trigger 3: *Alarm Event. Change proponents push too hard in implementing change, causing alarm among the status quo who begin to coalesce into their own subgroup.*

STAGE 4: Resistance. The status quo also coalesce into a group, while the change proponents step up their efforts to overcome this resistance to change.

Trigger 4: *Polarizing Event. Emotional intensity peaks as controversial decisions are made that drive apart the two groups. Many times the status quo succeeds in dismissing the pastor who, from their perspective, has failed to keep the change proponents in line.*

STAGE 5: Intense Conflict. Members of both the status quo and the change proponents expect other attendees to take sides.

Trigger 5: *Justifying Event. Both the change proponents and the status quo give ultimatums. Change proponents may threaten to leave unless change is implemented. The status quo often tells the change proponents that, if they want change, they should look elsewhere for a church. Each side does not perceive the other as demonstrating good will. One group prepares to exit, citing this event as the "justifi-cation" they needed to leave.*

STAGE 6: Group Exit. The rift between the change proponents and the status quo becomes so deep that one group, usually the change proponents, breaks away and exits the congregation.

The Stages of Group Exit When Accompanied by Positive Trigger Events

How will the course of group exit change if two of the negative trigger events are replaced with harmonizing and positive trigger events? The results can be astounding. Follow the group exit process below and see how radically the outcome differs when Trigger 2 and Trigger 4 are changed from negative events to positive events. It may seem remarkable, but research shows that simply changing these two trigger events can thwart group exits and deliberately and amicably bring about change in a church.[9] (Elements that are added to the above list are italicized for emphasis.)

STAGE 1: Relative Harmony.

Trigger 1: *Conflicting Ideas Event.* Some members attend a seminar or other idea-generating event where they get excited about new ideas that conflict with the church's customary way of operating.

STAGE 2: Idea Development. Individuals become convinced that the church is in need of change.

Trigger 2: *Positive Legitimating Event. Unlike the previous scenario, where the change proponents' ideas are inadvertently blessed, the process is now more planned, unhurried, and deliberate. In addition, the process is accompanied by prayer. Dialogue is encouraged, and permission is cautiously sought from the church leadership.*

STAGE 3: Change. The change proponents form a subgroup and implement change.

Trigger 3: *Alarm Event.* Change proponents push too hard for change, causing alarm among the status quo who begin to coalesce into their own subgroup.

STAGE 4: Resistance. The status quo also coalesce into a group, while the change proponents step up their efforts to overcome this resistance to change.

Trigger 4: Harmonizing Event. Unlike Trigger 4 in the earlier process, where controversial decisions drive apart the two groups, leaders now spend time listening and finding common ground. The focus is on organizational identity. In other words, the organization, rather than the subgroup, is celebrated. This results in a heightened sense of unity and a commitment to stick together. The results of this event or series of events are harmony, cohesiveness, and commitment to the larger organization.

STAGE 5: Dissonant Harmony. Though there is disagreement, there are no examples of highly emotional behavior, secret meetings, or suggestions that dissidents exit the congregation. Though some tension remains, as it will in all change processes, a high level of compromise is evident.

Trigger 5: The justifying event that thrusts people apart usually does not materialize.

STAGE 6: Group Retention. Rather than breaking away and exiting the congregation, the change proponents and status quo are retained. Because of the unifying nature of Trigger 2 (the positive legitimating event) and Trigger 4 (the harmonizing event), a new atmosphere of forbearance and lenience occurs. Harmonious relations, that still at times include a touch of dissonance, now guide congregational life.

Your Two Routes

In the rest of the book, you will find two different "routes" discussed in each chapter.

Route A, where negative triggering events #2 and #4 push people out of the church.

Route B, where positive versions of triggering events #2 and #4 keep change proponents and the status quo together in a congregation.

Where Do You Start?

Now that you have a brief overview of the group exit process, where should you start?

If You Are Not Currently Experiencing Group Exit

If you do not currently have a group exiting a church, you should take the chapters in the order they come. This way, you will receive a gradual appreciation and understanding of the dynamics involved in each step of the group exit process.

If You Are Currently Embroiled in Group Exit

If you are already ensnared in a group exit problem, you should skip ahead to the stage in the group exit process you are undergoing. To help discover which stage you are currently experiencing, ask yourself these questions.

QUESTIONS FOR GROUP STUDY, CHAPTER 2

Quickstart questions to help you decide where you are in the group exit process:

1. Though there has been some conflict in the past over new ideas, is the church presently experiencing a high degree of harmony? (If you answered "yes," proceed to chapter 3 and read the chapters in order. If you answered "no," proceed to the next question.)

2. Have some members recently been excited about some new ideas and especially eager to implement them? (If you answered "yes," proceed to chapter 6 and read the chapters

in order. When you have finished the book, go back and read chapters 3 to 5. If you answered "no," proceed to the next question.)

3. Have change proponents started to coalesce into a subgroup, started meeting separately, or are being recognized as an identifiable subgroup as they implement change? (If you answered "yes," proceed to chapter 7 and read the chapters in order. When you have finished the book, go back and read chapters 3 to 6. If you answered "no," proceed to the next question.)

4. Have the status quo started to coalesce into a recognizable subgroup to challenge changes and defend their traditions? Have the change proponents stepped up their efforts to overcome this resistance? (If you answered "yes" to either question, proceed to chapter 8 and read the chapters in order. When you have finished the book, go back and read chapters 3 to 7. If you answered "no," proceed to the next question.)

5. Have sides been taken over change resulting in, but not limited to, politicking, unpleasant letters, and meetings called to encourage alignment with either the status quo or change proponents? (If you answered "yes," proceed to chapter 9 and read the chapters in order. When you have finished the book, go back and read chapters 3 to 8. If you answered "no," proceed to the next question.)

6. Is a group currently on the verge of leaving the church over a significant disagreement over change? (If you answered "yes," proceed to chapter 10 and read the chapters in order. When you have finished the book, go back and read chapters 3 to 9. If you answered "no," proceed to the next question.)

7. Has a group recently left the church over change and there is little prospect of getting them to return? (If you answered "yes," proceed to chapter 6 and read the chapters in order. When you have finished the book, go back and read chapters 3 to 5.)

PART 1

HOW EXITS DESTROY CHURCHES

CHAPTER 3

The Pain (and Gain) of Exits

*Everything that irritates us about others can lead
us to an understanding of ourselves.*
—Carl G. Jung, psychologist[1]

The Pain of Exits

How Pastors Are Hit the Hardest

I had just completed a seminar on why people leave the church
over change. On the way out, I felt a hand grab my sleeve and,
out of the shadows appeared a well dressed but clearly uncomfortable gentleman in his midforties.

"Do you have a minute?" he began and, without waiting for the
reply, continued. "I know what you are talking about. I had three
successful church pastorates, all in a row. I was considered a success story in my denomination. But then I was appointed to North
Forest Church. I didn't know they were in the middle of what you
described as a conflict over change. The problem was that both
sides wanted me to keep the other in check. It's an impossible
job, and none of my training prepared me for this. I got caught
right in the middle, and I got sacked right away. Now the people
who wanted change are gone and the church is dying. What really
makes me frustrated is I feel like I'm blacklisted, because everyone thinks I destroyed North Forest Church."

I spent a few minutes trying to explain that it wasn't all his fault, that the church was caught in the middle of a six stage exit process. But, another exit had taken its toll and this time it was a dual exit of change proponents *and* the pastor.

The Emotional Turmoil That Erupts When People Leave a Church

Damage from group exits is not limited to pastors, for the congregation often suffers irreparable harm.

"I can see the church steeple every morning from my kitchen window," the distinguished-looking lady exclaimed. "And it hurts me to see what it's become," continued Mary. The church her parents had founded nearly eighty years ago sat in a cornfield on the outskirts of a growing college town. The slight hill on which the church sat made its steeple a visible landmark across the countryside. And, though this was once a little country church, full of proud farm families, it had recently been witnessing an influx of younger people as the town's suburbs penetrated the area. Soon, the newcomers attempted to bring about change more in keeping with their interests.

"They just wanted too much too soon. They wanted to get rid of our traditions, but our traditions are important to us. Those people wouldn't stop till they destroyed the church, and now they aren't even there anymore. We had to sell it because us old folks couldn't keep it up any longer. It's just a shame what happened, and it's because of them. I've lost the second most precious thing in my life, and every morning that steeple reminds me about it."

The psychological and spiritual damage to individuals is almost incalculable when a church slowly dies. While the influx of younger families should have meant a renaissance for the aging congregation, a lack of understanding of the forces involved resulted in the church's demise.

The Damage to Congregational Self-Image

The church had not experienced a group exit in almost a decade. So I was surprised when a man spoke up to lament the congregation's past failures at change. "We did all the stuff you people said," he interjected, "and look where it got us. We didn't keep the young people and we didn't grow. We've been limping along like this for eight years and we're too old to change. I think it's time we admitted we're as good as dead. Let's just close things up and go home!"

While many in the crowd did not share this gentleman's emotional intensity, the board voted to study their options. Six months later, I received a letter from the church moderator. In this letter she stated, "Dr. Whitesel, we appreciate your familiarization visit . . . but we think the best decision is to disband. . . . I think our people are just too wounded. And we don't think we can change without choosing sides."

Theologian and researcher Eddie Gibbs has said that "a congregation's level of expectation tends to be influenced more by past performance than by future prospects . . . [their] leadership is infected by a 'failure syndrome' which instantly attaches a lead weight to every kite which is flown."[2] And thus, because the change process is not well understood, a poor experience with change, even one almost a decade old, can thwart a church from trying to tackle change again.

Damage to a Church's Communitywide Image

The focus group was convened with nine members from the community who did not attend Hazel Street Church. Approximately halfway into the session, one gentleman summed up what the group had been hinting at. "The Hazel Street Church just doesn't have a good reputation. They've been pretty hard on their pastors. Everyone liked John Jenkins and we got to know him through Little League. It was just inexcusable what they did to him just because he wanted to bring in some new things. He was trying to get us to attend Hazel Street, and we just about did. Boy, am I glad we didn't! It's their reputation that is keeping people away."

"I knew people who left too," added one well-dressed woman in her midthirties. "They were really hard on those people (the change proponents) before they left. To me it doesn't seem like they practiced the Bible very much."

Until I changed the subject some ten minutes later, the remainder of the participants chimed in with similar concerns about the church's reputation. By mismanaging the change process, the church had created a communitywide negative image that obstructed potential growth.[3]

The Gain of Exits: When Exits Are Warranted

Mandy: An Unlikely Pastor

The church was a large congregation with attendance running more than three thousand. Frequently, groups of attendees would approach the leadership to ask for permission to start a daughter congregation. Due to the generous support of the mother church, both financially and emotionally, this was becoming a yearly occurrence. And with each successive offspring, the mother church seemed to gain back its lost members in new attendees.

"It was Mandy's group that wanted to leave," the pastor recalled. And this made the scenario different. Mandy was a deeply religious and passionate Christian. While he was admired by the leadership, his leanings were toward more emotional worship expressions than the mother church was comfortable with. In addition, the weeknight meeting he led had grown to more than four hundred attendees and consisted of a number of key leaders from the mother church.

As a result of Mandy's request, the decision was reached to offer Mandy an assistant pastorship in the parent organization. Prior to this he had only been a lay leader. Mandy and his associates prayerfully considered the proposal, but started their own congregation with a decidedly charismatic worship expression. The mother church reluctantly, but then unreservedly, supported the offspring.

Two years later, the mother church still ran about three thousand in attendance and the church Mandy pastored was nearing

1,200 attendees. The long-term result of this exit was a combined attendance of almost 4,500. In addition, two different church styles were now available in the community.

One Divided Church Gives Birth to
Two Healthy Congregations

"Hindsight is always 20/20. I can see now we were at the wrong place, trying to bring about things that would have destroyed their church." Almost a decade earlier, he had been part of a group that had tried to bring change to the church he grew up in.

"I don't think any of us realized the hornets' nest we were getting into," he continued. "Our Sunday school class was studying the role of women in the Bible. The stories of Deborah the judge, Pricilla, and others convinced us that the church's ban on female leaders was wrong. We had several talented women in our class, and they weren't allowed to lead it because they were female. It just seemed wrong and we thought it should be changed."

This gentleman's Sunday school class had grown to about twenty like-minded individuals. In a church with an attendance of approximately 150 this was a small, but significant, number. Needless to say, this class sent shock waves through the church.

Both sides, the change proponents and the status quo, politicked members to fortify their faction. But when the change proponents' ideas reached the denominational superintendent, the denomination mobilized its resources to quell the discussion. With permission from the status quo, the denomination officially disbanded and recolonized the congregation as a mission church. The leadership of the church was transferred to a regional committee of denominational officials and, as a result, the change proponents lost all administrative recourse.

Sensing the battle was lost and their input ineffectual, the change proponents exited the church. A nearby church with more accommodating views soon assimilated them. Almost ten years later, both churches are healthy: one with male-only leadership and the other, not surprisingly, with a female pastor.

Regardless of the reader's feelings about any leadership issues mentioned in the above two examples, the question that must be addressed is "When are group exits actually beneficial?" In these last two situations, the alterations the change proponents sought to bring about were clearly out of sync with the historical traditions and, in the second case, the denominational polity of the churches. In these scenarios, the exit of the change proponents into a church more in keeping with their beliefs was not only warranted but preferable, and could actually be looked at as gains for the Body of Christ.

To discover whether a group exit is warranted in your situation, visit the questions at the end of this chapter.

What If We Could Manage Change?

As you can see from the examples of painful exits, the mismanagement of change can often rob churches of its pastors, irreparably rend relationships, and undermine congregational self-image. Most of this misfortune is brought on by the mysterious nature of the change process.

But what if the change process were clearly understood as a sequence of "stages," and each stage had a specific "trigger event"? What if two trigger events could be adjusted slightly and, in most cases, a church could unite its change advocates and its status quo?

One of the most important principles of effective church management must be the successful supervision of the change process and the prevention of "painful" rather than "gainful" exits. Yet, there may be a silver lining to a congregation having experienced a prior painful exit: The church may now be more open to investigate and conquer the difficult mechanisms of change. Researchers at the Wharton School of Management found that most consumers only purchase home theft protection *after* they've been robbed.[4] So, too, it may be that churches will only tackle the elusive nature of change after they have been robbed of unity by a group exit.

QUESTIONS FOR GROUP STUDY, CHAPTER 3

Criteria to Decide If and When an Exit Is Warranted

Answer the following questions and then consult the scoring guide at the end of this section to interpret your answers.

1. Do change proponents want to incorporate practices or beliefs that run counter to a historical denominational policy and/or doctrine? Examples:

    • Adult baptism in a church that historically recognizes only infant baptism;
    • Female leadership in a church whose denominational affiliation does not support such leadership;
    • Pentecostal or charismatic expressions (speaking in tongues, prophesy, etc.) in a church that has denominational prohibitions against such practices;

2. Do the status quo quickly digress to personal attacks, name-calling, and taunts when confronted with change? In other words, are the members of the status quo rigidly and emotionally opposed to change?

3. Do the change proponents quickly digress to personal attacks, intimidation, and taunts when trying to bring about change? In other words, are change proponents inflexible and fanatically committed to change?

4. Is the church severely weakened by financial, relational, or denominational problems that have the potential to close the church in the foreseeable future? For example:

    • Has a scandal (financial, spiritual, or sexual) rocked the church so much that there is doubt about the church's ability to survive?

- Have legal problems put the future of the church in jeopardy?
- Is the viability of the church facility in jeopardy? Will the church soon be forced to relocate or conduct extensive renovations that endanger its fiscal viability?

Scoring Guide: How to Interpret Your Answers

If you answered *yes* to two or more of the above questions, then your congregation should unhurriedly and carefully investigate whether change is advisable at the present time. It may be, in your circumstances, that an exit of change proponents may be in the interest not only of long-term church health, but the spiritual health of the status quo and the change proponents as well.

CHAPTER 4

A Tale of One Church in Two Parts

There are people who, instead of solving a problem, tangle it up and make it harder to solve for anyone who wants to deal with it. Whoever does not know how to hit the nail on the head should not be asked to hit it at all.

—Friedrich Nietzsche, philosopher[1]

Southeast Church, Part 1: Battle Lines Are Drawn

As we left the congregational meeting, the pastor leaned heavily against his wife. Despite her petite frame, she bore the weight of his body, an action that seemed strangely parallel to the emotional strength she had provided to this hulk of a man for more than four years. As we left, she turned to me and sighed, "Why do they do this? He just tried to do what they wanted." Not knowing how to respond, I remained silent, but as Jim and his wife left the building he softly told me, "They don't want to change, they'll never change."

The church had once been a vibrant congregation in an inner suburb of a metropolitan community. In the 1970s, the members had been more than four hundred strong. Now they were a shadow of their former self. The denomination had decided this church needed a strong hand to change their direction, and appointed a determined, yet likable, leader. They didn't realize it, but this pastor was headed into a hopeless situation where his personality would only exacerbate the situation until he and the church would be estranged.

Jim had been the voice of progress and change in two former associate pastorships. In both positions he had helped plateaued churches reach out to new ethnic groups moving into the neighborhood. In fact, in this denomination Jim was something of a sensation.

To the denominational hierarchy, sending Jim to Southeast Church was the best scenario. Southeast had been a prestigious church that had plateaued due to a changing ethnicity in the community. Southeast Church seemed like the ideal fit for Jim.

Initially, Change Advocates Are Welcome

The church had welcomed Jim and his family with open arms. But things started to go awry. Early in his tenure, many of the leaders met with Jim and expressed their readiness to see the church change. They had witnessed more than twenty years of declining numbers, and they knew they must do something to return to the glory days. As a result of these conversations, Jim received the impression that he had carte blanche to proceed with change initiatives.

Jim was impressed with the leaders' willingness to change. "The people who wanted things to stay the same seemed almost nonexistent," he confided to me years later. "I thought that this would be the place where I would finish my career." Instead, Southeast turned out to be a very different experience, one that nearly spiritually bankrupted Jim.

Polarization Begins: Yellow Lights Instead of Green Lights

How did this disintegration take place? The seeds of failure were sown in the intial communication from the church leaders. The church leaders were so optimistic about saving the church by implementing change, they gave Jim a false impression of their readiness to inaugurate the change. They were more intellectually prepared to embrace change than they were emotionally. Once Jim industriously began the change process, the church leaders started to feel uncomfortable, even downright hesitant, to support the new ideas they felt were being implemented too soon and too fast.

Jim, however, thought he had received unmistakable permission for such a radical overhaul of the church's ministry. The problem was that the actual expectations of the church leaders were somewhat less radical than their verbal statements. While Jim thought he had a green light, he only had a yellow light to "proceed cautiously."

But since Jim took the church's leaders at their spoken word, he threw caution to the wind and flung his considerable talents into bringing about change at the earliest opportunity.

Jim had scarcely been at the church two months when he took some of the church's key leaders to a seminar on how to start a modern worship service.[2] The leaders were handpicked by Jim to reflect the most progressive lay leaders in the church. Only one leader was invited from the status quo. Jim felt the ideas that the seminar would germinate were of little interest to the status quo, so he thought no more of their participation.

The Triggering Event: Too Much, Too Soon

Jim and the leaders came back from the seminar with a burning desire to see a modern worship service initiated at Southeast. Demonstrating an all too typical infatuation with technology, Jim and other leaders began pressuring the church for a new sound system, a video-projector, and an electronic keyboard. These are expensive items, and soon this church that had suffered from tightening budgets for more than two decades was inundated with requests for substantial spending. Such requests made the status quo, who often populated the financial committees, skittish and hesitant. Slowly and almost imperceptibly, they began to dig in their heels to slow the unbridled progress.

Jim and his supporters felt betrayed. The church leaders had unreservedly communicated that they wanted change, and in his mind they had reneged on their promise. How could a church leadership that so openly and publicly solicited change now thwart the process?

Everything Jim read seemed to indicate that culture is

changing so rapidly that you must move ahead at the fastest possible clip. With the summer approaching, he announced that a new modern service would begin on a trial basis, secretly hoping that this summer service would become a regular fixture in the fall. His tactics did not go unnoticed by the status quo.

Soon, a modern service was under way. Since Jim and other change proponents launched this new worship alternative without appropriate sound systems, video-projectors, or musical instruments, the quality of the service was not up to anyone's expectations. The musicians were inexperienced in this new format and Jim found himself and his family doing most of the work. The status quo, looked with bewilderment on the lack of organization in the modern service.

From Polarization to Separation:
A Pastor Caught in the Middle

It was not long before the modern service had caused considerable tension over its lack of proficiency. Jim and his confederates blamed the status quo for verbally supporting change and then refusing to fund it. The status quo, on the other hand, felt Jim had failed in his duties. They had seen him as an agent who would keep the change proponents in check while bringing about change in a manner that did not alienate the status quo.

Change proponents saw Jim as unable to convince the status quo about the necessity of change. The status quo saw Jim as unable to keep the change proponents in line. Jim was caught in the middle.

To address the dilemma, a meeting of the church membership was called. Sensing a showdown over change, Jim decided to launch a series of sermons that would bolster his and the change proponents' position. He hammered home the importance of change in the survival of the church. After four weeks of sermons, the church meeting convened.

The illustration that began this chapter was the aftermath of this meeting. Jim had been publicly chastised for not keeping the change proponents in check, and the change proponents returned the volleys by attacking the credibility and honesty of the status quo. Jim, a man of deep piety and spirituality, could not stand to see the church torn apart. About three hours into the meeting, with his wife by his side and his children looking on, Jim resigned. This was the first major defeat in Jim's career, and it resonated to the very core of his being. Unsure about his call to ministry, Jim accepted a position in the administrative arm of the denomination. But the incident left scars, and both the church and its former leader were left with a feeling of failure.

Southeast Church, Part 2: A Survival Story

Dr. Thompson was not my first choice for an interim pastor after Jim's departure. I had envisioned a younger pastor who could lead the church back to health. It was not that Dr. Thompson lacked faith or spirituality; he embodied both. And it was not that he was inexperienced; he had led a large, but aging, congregation in the inner city for more than a decade. It was just that his unhurried demeanor was not what I had envisioned for Southeast Church. Happily, the denominational leaders did not share my assessment of the situation. Before long, Dr. Thompson would demonstrate that he was a leader who could unite a polarized church.

Dr. Thompson's tenure began much the same as Jim's. Dr. Thompson gathered a group of church leaders and accompanied them to a denominationally sponsored seminar on church growth. However, Dr. Thompson diverted from Jim's strategy by including a broad spectrum of attendees from both the status quo and the change proponents. When members of the status quo initially declined his offer, he coaxed them into attending. Initially, this action looked like it would only further polarize the congregation, giving each side more ammunition with which to attack one another. But Dr. Thompson's strategy soon became clear.

Once back from the seminar, many members braced for what they feared would be another uncomfortable conflict between the change proponents and the status quo. The seminar had been stimulating for both factions, and each found ideas they embraced and others they disparaged, mostly on opposite ends of the spectrum. Dr. Thompson was expected to wade into the escalating fray, but something unexpected happened.

Patience, Prayer, and Unity Share Center Stage

Dr. Thompson announced that he was going to take several weeks to pray about the proposals suggested at the seminar and would not be talking about the issues until he had clear direction from the Lord. He told the congregants that he hoped they would join him in this time of focus, reflection, and petition. The best plans, he said, were those that had the unmistakable hand of the Lord upon them.

For the next three weeks, the change proponents and status quo worked together to keep the everyday ministries of the church running. In all areas of the church, the unifying practices that had bound the people together for years now shared center stage.

Sharing this spotlight was also a heightened emphasis on prayer. Groups of the change proponents gathered for prayer, as did groups of the status quo. But because talk about church growth strategies was not yet encouraged, these gatherings focused on intent and not tactics.

At the culmination of several weeks, Dr. Thompson suggested the congregation should now engage in conversations on growth, as well as continue in prayer. During this time, informal and formal discussions began to take place. Surprisingly cordial, bipartisan discussions on the topic of strategic growth emerged.

Both sides seemed somewhat surprised that they had so much in common. Both wanted the church to survive, both wanted to reach unchurched and dechurched people, and both wanted to keep the existing membership intact. Without a deadline looming and with time to ruminate over the ideas gleaned from the seminar, both sides ignored tactics and began to discover common ground on long-range intent. At the end of another three weeks, there was a decidedly unified atmosphere in the congregation.

Next, Dr. Thompson announced that he had formulated his

own opinions. During a church council meeting, he shared ideas that closely paralleled the ideas that had been germinated in the bipartisan meetings of the past few weeks. He then suggested that a church leadership retreat be held to formulate plans for the future. The leaders wholeheartedly embraced the retreat, seeing it as a time to further define the moderated ideas they had been discussing in bipartisan groups.

Within six months, Southeast decided to sell the church building. Selecting a site a few miles away, they began to plan a modern service along the lines of Pastor Jim's vision. But now the plans had gained a widespread acceptance, and they had been carefully and diligently designed by a bipartisan leadership team that had prayerfully considered their options.

This is not to say that some tensions did not arise. With change, tension is inevitable; but Dr. Thompson seemed to anticipate this.

Dr. Thompson began a series of sermons on the history of Southeast Church. Though highly anticipated by the status quo, the change proponents had less interest in the topic. But, because the church only had one service, the change proponents felt obligated to attend.

Finding Unity in the Past

Over the next several weeks, Dr. Thompson relived the history of the church, purposely focusing on the role of change in the church's history. He pointed out that the church had been founded as an outreach to the growing suburbs more than eighty years ago. At the time, the church had been an offshoot of an urban mother church that wished to reach the new suburban dwellers. As a result, Southeast wholeheartedly embraced new approaches to ministry to reach its suburban neighbors.

When Dr. Thompson finished his sermon series, his listeners had a renewed sense of change, vision, and unity. Both the status quo and the change proponents realized that tensions over change had always existed, but the church had survived and even thrived.

The church began to stress its organizational identity rather than the identity of its factions. The change proponents had wanted to change the church's name from "Southeast [denominational name] Church," to something more contemporary. Of course, for the status quo the illustrious history of the church was embodied in its name. However, after a series of bipartisan meetings the name was changed to simply "Southeast Church," with the denominational designation in a byline. The result was a new name, "Southeast Church: A [denominational name] Congregation," concurrently stressed both the historical, organizational, and modern identity of the congregation.

Harmonizing and Unhurried Leadership

The outcome of Dr. Thompson's leadership was that crucial changes at Southeast Church were enacted. Dr. Thompson, in his gentle and unifying manner, had helped the church adopt change in a way that was both unhurried and harmonious.

The strategic step was the appointment of Dr. Thompson. He had the foresight and experience to know that the church had to move forward, but that doing so in an unhurried manner and unifying manner would bring together the change proponents and the status quo in purpose and direction.

The Difference Between Southeast Church Parts 1 and 2

As you can see from the first part of the story, there was a series of well-intentioned missteps by the pastor in the change process. It was these mistakes that differentiated the outcomes for Part 1 and Part 2. Let's review these subtle, yet crucial missteps.

- **Misstep #1:** The pastor listened to the well-intentioned words of the status quo rather than their hearts. While most members of the status quo recognized the need for change, the rapidity and comprehensive nature of Pastor Jim's change was disconcerting.

- **Misstep #2:** Pastor Jim's sermon series that was intended to bring about support for change did the opposite. The purpose of the sermons was to legitimize his new ideas, but it did little to convince the status quo of their appropriateness. As a result, the sermons only drove the change proponents and status quo into two separate camps. By the time the congregational meeting was held, the two groups were so polarized that fireworks erupted. And Jim got burned.

Part 2 of Southeast Church's story contains progressive and unifying actions at two crucial junctures that avoided the missteps of Part 1. Let's recap two steps in Part 2 that led to a different outcome.

- **Proactive Step #1:** Dr. Thompson actively included the status quo in the planning of change. He also gave each side time to pray and informally discuss the suitability and adaptability of the new ideas within bipartisan discussion.

- **Proactive Step #2:** After customary tensions arose over the change process, Dr. Thompson inaugurated a sermon series that focused on the inevitability of change along with the historical similarities between the status quo and the change proponents. He fostered harmony within the congregation. In addition, the organizational identity was emphasized rather than the individual identity of either subgroup.

In the following chapters, the reader will see how the missteps of Part 1 can be avoided by understanding them as the negative trigger events that further polarize members of a congregation. In addition, the proactive steps of Part 2 will be seen as the positive trigger events that cultivate dialogue and harmony. If the negative trigger events of Part 1 are replaced with the positive trigger events of Part 2, a church can forestall polarization and slowly, but purposefully, inaugurate change. Chapters 5 through 11 will address this process in detail.

QUESTIONS FOR GROUP STUDY, CHAPTER 4:

Are You Headed Toward Southeast Church Part 1 or Part 2?

1. Can you recall a time in the past where your leaders or attendees verbally supported change, only to withdraw that support when ideas were introduced too quickly or too extensively? What was the outcome?

2. Have change proponents and the status quo polarized in your church through subtle name-calling, finger pointing, and questioning of motives? What was the outcome?

3. What was the aftermath from the last idea-generating or leadership seminar your leaders attended? Were ideas carefully considered and unhurriedly solidified, or was there a rush to implement plans and programs? In hindsight, what would you have done differently?

4. When tensions began to arise over new ideas, does the congregation focus on finding common ground, stressing organizational identity as well as celebrating their shared aims? Can you give three examples?

5. Have you listed the goals of the change proponents as well as the status quo, looking for agreement? If not, why not start a list of goals held by each group, looking for shared objectives. Can you list five?

6. Over the past decade, has the church experienced any pastoral transitions where disagreement over the degree or rapidity of change was a factor? In hindsight, how might the situation be handled differently?

PART 2

How People Exit a Church in Six Stages

CHAPTER 5

Stage 1: Relative Harmony

*I want relations which are not purely personal, based on
purely personal qualities; but relations based upon some
unanimous accord in truth or belief, and a harmony of purpose,
rather than of personality. I am weary of personality.*
—D. H. Lawrence, author[1]

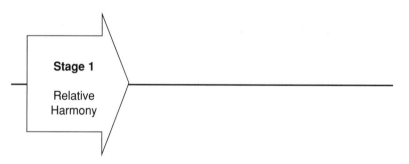

Stage 1

Relative
Harmony

Stage 1: Lulled into Complacency

"At times in the past, we were all together," declared the diminutive lady. "We didn't have these conflicts over music and styles." Other heads began to nod in affirmation across the room. In this meeting of church leaders, the conversation had gently, but decidedly, turned to past unity. Many of those in attendance lamented how new ideas in music and worship were making the status quo feel uncomfortable. Many of those in attendance privately and openly lamented the loss of simpler times, when the church was at peace.

In the front row, a prominent lay leader in his late forties asked permission to read a portion from the church's celebrated history. "In October of 1824, a few people gathered in a log cabin in our town to worship," he began. "In 1829, the first formal church was organized just west of where the hotel now stands. In 1841, ours was the first church building erected in town. In 1867, an organ was purchased for use in the church, over protests of the choir leader who called it a 'thing of the devil.' "[2]

This story aptly illustrates how hindsight is rarely 20/20. In retrospect, periods of congregational peace may seem more harmonious than they actually were. And these target years of concord and serenity become a golden era for many churches that they wish to regain. Such eras do occur, but they are perhaps not as tension free as remembered.

Stage 1: Relative Harmony

A DEFINITION

There are times when churches experience periods of relative tranquillity and serenity, going about their congregational life somewhat free of polarizing conflict. Sometimes imagined, but occasionally real, we will label this period "Stage 1." This stage is a wonderful period where church-going ceases to be a chore and becomes a pleasure as the church lives out its testimony in the world with relative unity and accord.

Stage 1: Relative Harmony. In this stage a congregation exhibits the three "C's."
  1. *Contented.* Congregants are relatively content or satisfied with the church's ministries, direction, and purpose.
  2. In *Concord.* The congregation focuses more on what holds them together than what pulls them apart.
  3. There is some *Conflict.* Conflict and tensions occasionally arise, but the congregation works to keep them from causing division. This is why this stage is labeled "relative" harmony.

SOME CHARACTERISTICS OF STAGE 1: RELATIVE HARMONY

Characteristics of Stage 1 include (but are not limited to) the following:

- Most members are relatively satisfied with the church's purpose and how it is being fulfilled.
- There is a general perception that church attendees are working together and united in purpose.
- This period is sometimes recalled as "the good old days."
- However, this harmony is labeled relative because there is usually some tension over the inevitable changes that are taking place.

As satisfying as Stage 1 can be, it can easily mask emerging complacency.

Lulled into Complacency at Long Street Church

After the meeting I stood in a reception line alongside the pastor who had guided this church for fifteen years. One gentleman summed up what had been stated in various ways in the meeting that evening: "I appreciate the work you do Dr. Whitesel. But we've been a model of a strong church for years. I don't think we've got much to be worried about." The pastor leaned over to me a few minutes later and remarked "that's an example of what's wrong. They're dying and they don't know it."

A casual conversation in the fellowship hall a few minutes later threw more light on the situation. A mature lady tendered a long and storied perspective. "You don't know us," she eventually summarized. "It takes a long time to increase the size of a church, and just to stay at this size is a mighty big accomplishment. We've even had two churches join us. We keep staying strong and I don't think there is much chance of us needing help."

She was right in several aspects. The church had received new members when two smaller congregations were disbanded and the members were encouraged to join Long Street Church. To members of the denomination, it seemed like Long Street Church was a safe haven. Its stately granite walls and central location in the town seemed to ooze security. Unrecognized by many of the lay leaders, but not by the pastor, was the fact that the church was not keeping up with their town's population growth.

This perspective was confirmed by a phone call I received two weeks later by a local businessman who was a lay leader in the congregation. "We've got big problems here at Long Street," he began. "The community is growing and the businesses know it." He continued to describe how this midsized town was becoming a bedroom community for a metropolitan area some forty miles to the northeast.

This community had been insulated from the effects of urban sprawl for many years. However, now long-range commuters had reached this community. First they came in a trickle. And because the influx was modest, the growth was overlooked by most of the area's churches.

"I told the pastor what I was seeing. We [business people] are having our sales increase dramatically," the layman explained. "It's being driven by the newcomers from the city," he continued. "I told the pastor and he's open to the idea of hiring a consultant. Perhaps you can convince our leaders."

Soon afterward, the pastor and the lay leader convened a meeting. The first twenty minutes of the meeting were consumed with comments of bewilderment as to why Long Street Church should need help. The church had maintained an attendance of approximately two hundred attendees for the past three decades. To most of the leaders, the future of the church looked secure.

The church did have many things in its favor, but these traits also kept the church's leadership from gaining an accurate picture of the situation. In the church's favor were the following:

- The church had received an influx of members from two disbanded congregations in the 1970s and 1980s.
- The church had maintained a size of approximately two hundred attendees for more than three decades.
- The church's consistent size also made it a model church within the denomination. As a result, Long Street Church hosted many denominational forums and workshops.
- The church's size of approximately two hundred attendees

conveyed the picture that it was better off than 85 percent of the churches in America.[3]

Even though the above traits seemed to forecast a healthy and happy future, the population figures revealed a gradual, but steady, erosion of the church's size in comparison to the population of the community. Population figures, readily available from the U.S. Census Bureau, helped the leaders understand this picture. Utilizing simple formulas—such as those in figures 5.1, 5.2, and 5.3—the leaders were able to compare their attendance growth with the growth in the surrounding community.

The lay leaders concluded, and I concurred, that the church should be experiencing growth that is at least equal to the growth of the community's population.

Figures 5.1, 5.2, and 5.3 demonstrate how you can compare your church's attendance growth to the population growth in the surrounding community. Uncovering a church's growth patterns, or lack thereof, and comparing it to a community's growth pattern is a straightforward, three-part process.

The numbers used in figures 5.2, 5.3, and 5.4 are actual numbers from a congregation. Their leaders felt they were "holding their own" but the local businessman knew they were falling behind community growth.

Further analysis of Long Street's locale revealed that community planners were anticipating a 20 percent increase in the population over the next ten years, as rail service to the metropolitan area was updated. The prognosis for this community was good, but the church leadership was largely unaware of their lackluster track record or of their potential.

At the same time, two denominations without congregations in the community targeted the area for new church starts. Many times, when new churches are planted in an area, all churches will benefit from a renewed interest in religion in the community. However, these church plantings should have been a wake-up call to Long Street Church that the harvest of souls that Jesus described in John 4:35 as "gleaming white, all ready for the harvest" (JBP) was already under way in their community.

Figure 5.1

Part 1: *How to determine the* change in population *for your community*

1. To determine the population of your community, go to the U.S. Census Bureau Web site at *www.census.gov* and click on the "search" button.
2. From there you will have several options for attaining 1990 and 2000 census data for your community.
3. Next, find the change in community population for your area. This is done with a very simple equation:

$$\frac{\textit{Population change} \text{ (between first year and last year)}}{\text{Population of 1st year being studied}} = \frac{x}{100}$$

EXAMPLE:

(Subtract from the last year figure, the first year number to get the *population change* between first year and last year.)

$$\begin{array}{r} \text{Population in 2000} = 8574 \\ -\text{ Population in 1990} = 7462 \\ \hline \textit{Population Change} = 1112 \end{array}$$

$$\frac{\textit{Population Change}}{\text{Population of first year}} = \frac{x}{100}$$

$$\frac{1112}{7462} = \frac{x}{100}$$

x = 14.9% growth in community population

4. Write down the change in community population for future reference.

Figure 5.2
Part 2: *How to determine the* change in attendance
for your church.[4]

1. Write down the church attendance for the first year of the period being studied. Example = 202

2. Then write down the church membership for the last year of the period being studied. Example = 199

3. Next, find the change in church membership or attendance for your congregation. This is done with the same equation used in Figure 5.1:

$$\frac{\textit{Attendance change}\text{ (between first year and last year)}}{\text{Attendance of first year being studied}} = \frac{x}{100}$$

EXAMPLE:
(Subtract from the last year figure, the first year number to get the *attendance change* between first year and last year.)

$$
\begin{array}{ll}
& \text{Attendance in 2000} = 199 \\
- & \underline{\text{Attendance in 1990} = 202} \\
& \textit{Attendance Change}\ --3
\end{array}
$$

$$\frac{\textit{Attendance change}}{\text{Attendance of first year}} = \frac{x}{100}$$

$$\frac{-3}{202} = \frac{x}{100}$$

$$x = -1.5\% \text{ growth in attendance}$$

4. Write down the change in attendance for future reference.

Figure 5.3: *How to determine the difference between the* change in attendance *for your church and the* change in community population.

Subtact the lesser number from the larger number to get the difference between the percentage of growth in a community and the percentage of growth in a church.

EXAMPLE:

Change in Community Population =   14.9%
Change in Attendance   = − −1.5%[5]
DIFFERENCE   =   16.4%

The church in the above example thought it had plateaued because it was hovering around two hundred attendees over the past ten years. However, when compared to the growth in the community's population, it had lost a whopping 16 percent of the share of the community. In other words, ten years ago the congregation had a 16 percent greater proportion of the community attending their church than they now have.

How Generational Changes Create Complacency

In our Quickstart Guide of chapter 2, we looked at the four generations that comprise society. They range in age from the Builders all the way down to Generation Y.

These generations have different needs and expectations in a church. A Generation X couple may look for a church with a good nursery and Sunday school for their children. Boomers may seek out classes on parenting teens, or marriage seminars. Builders may need opportunities to gather with a dwindling circle of friends for extended discussions and conversation.

Because different generations have different needs in a church, a church that is organized and led by leaders of one dominant generation may inadvertently create ministries that are not attractive to other age groups. For example, a church with mostly

Builder leadership will naturally create ministries that are attractive to other Builders. A vicious circle can result—Builders create programming that is intended to reach Boomers but, because it is designed by Builders, it often attracts only more Builders. As a result, the Boomers, to whom the baton of leadership must eventually be passed, feel ignored and go elsewhere.

Complacency begins when the age group that is designing outreach begins to rationalize away why its outreach programs have failed. The initiating group often attributes the programs' failure to the lack of openness on the part of the respondents. Not understanding generational differences and preferences, the older generation gives up its outreach tactics, citing that the problem is not with the programs, but with the lack of receptivity in their targeted audience. Actually, the failure may be because those creating the outreach are out of touch with the needs of the targeted age group. But by charging that the targeted age group is insensitive and uninterested, the initiating generation can absolve its conscience and become complacent.

Figure 5.4 offers a brief overview of some major differences in programming that are often needed by different generations. For a fuller discussion of what each generation is looking for in a church, see chapter 3, "Attitudes that Produce the Gaps," in *A House Divided*.

It is clear from figure 5.4 that different generations have different needs that a church must be prepared to meet. If the community around the church is changing in age and the church is still programming for an older and dwindling generation, complacency may arise and put that church in jeopardy.

How Ethnic Changes Create Complacency

A similar complacency can occur when the presence of an ethnic group, that is different from a church's historical ethnicity, increases in the community. Often, a growing ethnic group will have different cultural preferences.

At first, a church will wonder how it can reach out to an ethnic group growing nearby. Many churches, however, will soon dispense with this option, feeling that the cultural differences are too

Figure 5.4

What Different Generations Are Looking for in a Church

Generation	Church Personality	Denomination	Ministries
Builder (born in and before 1945)	* Traditional worship * Leader presents ideas * New ideas are cautiously studied * Change is accepted when it fits in with the church's personality	* Mainline affiliation	* Fellowship usually takes place in larger groups * Traditional programs such as choir, women's societies, etc. * Lecture format preferred in Bible studies and Sunday school
Boomer (born between 1946 and 1964)	* Modern worship with contemporary musical instruments: keyboards, guitars, world (i.e. international) instruments * Emphasis on personal growth * Leader facilitates ideas * New ideas are encouraged, studied, and embraced	* Interdenominational affiliation, or a mainline-church with a nondenominational feel	* Fellowship in medium-sized groups * Programs in parenting, finances, marriage, etc. * Leadership development is stressed * Cooperative format preferred in Bible studies and Sunday school, where questions are encouraged

Generation X (born between 1965 and 1983)	* Postmodern worship, with movie clips, etc. * Practical sermons with "take-away" value * Attendees facilitate ideas * New ideas are experimented with, often without formal approval	* Some denominational affiliation is sought due to the stability it provides * However, affiliation does not matter as much as up-to-date programming	* Small groups that provide intimacy * Debate format preferred in Bible studies and Sunday school, where attendees are encouraged to share apprehensions
Generation Y (born between 1984 and 2001)	* Worship that utilizes new technology, such as the Internet, personal digital assistants (PDAs) video, and computers * Technology facilitates ideas * New ideas are technology-driven, thus formal approval or participation by others is not needed	* Still too early to say, but they seem to be leaning toward denominational affiliation because of the stability it affords	* Fellowship in medium-sized groups (though this may change to small groups as they enter their twenties) * Technology-driven ministries, such as: online Bible studies, Internet prayer circles, online board meetings, etc. * Technological format preferred in Bible studies, with online research * Technological format pre-ferred in Bible studies

divergent to create any common ground. In such circumstances, many churches will be lulled into complacency by thinking that nothing can be done. Seeing no viable options, they will limp along, resigning themselves to a slow and painful death.

But there is hope! Many churches in communities where ethnicity is changing have discovered the advantages of having churches of different cultures meet in the same building. One such approach, called the key church strategy, suggests a "key" or anchor church becomes host for various satellite churches of different ethnicities within its building.[6] Already, in many metropolitan areas, it is not uncommon to see a Hispanic congregation meeting at 8 A.M., a Korean congregation at 11 A.M., and a Chinese congregation in the evening—all within the same key church. These examples remind us that changes in the ethnicity of a community do not need to create complacency.

The Inevitable Question: Will the Church Conquer Complacency?

What, then, is the recourse for a church that feels it is in Stage 1 (relative harmony), when it is actually losing ground due to population increases or changes in the generational or ethnic culture surrounding the church?

The recourse is change—a change that is studied, planned, and circumspectly implemented so that it occurs without dividing the status quo from the change proponents. As the reader will see in the following chapter, change brings about tension and this tension often results in polarization and group exit.

If a church is to survive the change process, the leaders must know the mechanics involved in successfully navigating and implementing change. One of the most strategic junctures is the next stage, Stage 2 where new ideas are introduced and how the church responds to them.

QUESTIONS FOR GROUP STUDY, CHAPTER 5

Are You In (or Headed Into) STAGE 1: Relative Harmony?

1. Do your members wish to return to the "good old days"?
   - Were these glory days as conflict free as they are remembered? (You may have to do some investigating.)
   - If not, are there parallels with current conflicts?

2. Has the community surrounding your church been growing faster than church attendance? If it has, return to figures 5.1, 5.2, and 5.3 in this chapter.

3. Does your community possess a growing age group that is not represented proportionally within your church?
   - If this is the case, use the process outlined in figure 5.1 to visit the U.S. Census Bureau Web site. There you can obtain the size of the age groups in your area.
   - Tabulate percentages in your community for Builders, Boomers, Generation X, and Generation Y.
   - Poll your church attendees to determine the church's percentages of Builders, Boomers, Generation X, and Generation Y.[7]
   - Compare these percentages. A healthy multi-generational church will have generational percentages that are proportional to the community.

4. Is the ethnicity of the community changing? If it is, ask yourself the following:
   - Has the church lost interest in reaching out to an emerging ethnicity because of past failures?
   - Has the church had some successes with outreach efforts to

this new ethnicity? If yes, list them. Are any of them capable of being revised?

- What are other churches doing in the area that is effectively reaching out to this new ethnicity? Could you do this also?

CHAPTER 6

Stage 2: When New Ideas Are Introduced

*There is nothing more difficult to take in hand, more perilous
to conduct, or more uncertain in its success, than to
take the lead in the introduction of a new order of things.*
—Niccolo Machiavelli, political theorist[1]

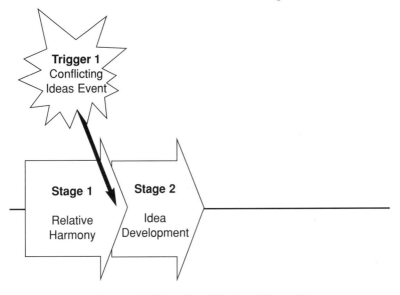

Trigger 1: The Conflicting Ideas Event

The Usual (and Divisive) Ways New Ideas Are Introduced

"Stand up!" instructed the seminar leader. "Now yell it at the top of your voice: Give us, Lord, new wine!" After the phrase was shouted two more times, the meeting adjourned.

These church leaders had gathered from across the region to hear about the latest trends in modern worship. These ideas were put forth by a respected leader and author. It was clear the topic had deep personal meaning for those in attendance, but this room had almost taken on the ambiance of a political rally aimed at replacing traditional forms of worship with modern expressions.[2]

The seminar's theme was based on Matthew 9:17, where Jesus urged his followers to "pour new wine into new wineskins." The "new wine" analogy had been applied to modern forms of worship throughout the seminar, and traditional forms of worship were designated the "old wineskins." An audience member could not help but retain an image of God's preference for new wine.

In the biblical context of this parable, Jesus pointed out that new wine (the new understanding Jesus brought) would tear or damage old wineskins (John's traditions), for they were two different entities. However, the last verse of the parable seemed to be overlooked by those attending the seminar. In the conclusion, Jesus suggested "they pour new wine into new wineskins, *and both are preserved*" (v. 17, italics mine). The lesson seems to be, in part, that both new wineskins and old wineskins are valuable and are to be preserved. But in the seminars, this broader thesis seemed overlooked, resulting in the belittling of traditional worship forms. I wholeheartedly support the validity of all expressions of worship: modern, postmodern, and traditional. In my earlier book, I have demonstrated how these expressions can peacefully coexist in the same congregation.[3]

But, what had begun to worry me about the current seminar was that it was not a case of "both/and" in this seminar, but an argument for "either/or." The animated and passionate ending to the seminar had bothered me by its deprecation of traditional forms of worship in an attempt to increase appreciation for more modern manifestations.

Granted, very few worship seminars culminate this way. But the pep rally conclusion to these seminars may have headed the participants down a road that would eventually lead to the failure of their attempt to bring about changes in worship.

"YOU'VE GOT TO READ THIS!"

About a year earlier, I had facilitated a meeting for members of a church council who had sent six of their leaders to a seminar on small groups. The seminar leader was a respected author, who had challenged churches that were not growing to consider adopting the cell church model of ministry.

This approach stressed the value of small groups as the foundational structure of a church.[4] Some churches had even eliminated weekly corporate worship services to focus on more intimate worship once a week in small groups. These "cell churches," as they are sometimes called, have much to commend them. They re-create the milieu of first-century Christianity where most worship, accountability, and intimacy took place in small house groups. While there was nothing wrong with the cell group approach, there was something wrong with the way the seminar attendees sought to introduce it back at their home church.

"You've got to read this!" one lay leader exclaimed about a book he had purchased at the seminar. "It's revolutionized my life! It is what we need, I have no doubt about it." A few minutes later, he concluded his praise by declaring, "You're just not ready for a deeper experience unless you read this book."

This illustrates how it is often neither the content nor the purveyor that is at fault, but the local messenger. This local lay leader was primed for overstatement. He had been worried for some time about the dwindling numbers of attendees at his church. To him, small groups appeared to be the lifeline that might reconnect this dwindling church with God. These ideas seemed to be the last-ditch hope for a church that was slowly taking on water and poised to disappear beneath the waves of cultural change.

Sometimes, it is a book, other times, it is a seminar, audiotape, videotape, or lecture that becomes the perceived instrument of rescue. Either way, an instrument of instruction mutates into an instrument of partition.

Before we continue with another illustration, it is important to recall that new ideas are often not injurious in and of themselves, but they are often only inappropriately presented. That is why, throughout this book, we will be looking at "exit antidotes," actions that can prevent exit behavior and elicit change. Here is our first.

Exit Antidote 1: New ideas are usually germinated from a sincere desire to see a church increase or improve its ministry. Rarely, but on occasion (see the disclaimer in chapter 7), do people suggest change simply for the sake of newness. Most often, church attendees seek to implement new ideas because they genuinely believe change will augment and expand a church's ministry. Keep in mind this goodhearted motivation, and be careful not to disparage new ideas because of the discomfort that newness always conveys. If you are uncomfortable with ideas being proposed, give them some initial latitude and spend time in prayer regarding them. Ask God to change your opinion or their point of view. Often the fruit of new ideas and/or of prayer can help change, or moderate perspectives. (See chapter 6 for details.)

"AT FOREST CREEK CHURCH, WE DID THINGS DIFFERENTLY."

Everyone was growing more uncomfortable as the night progressed. The night had appeared promising at the onset, but one gentleman began to dominate the conversation.

"At Forest Creek Church, we did things differently. And it was difficult for a lot of people. But, in time, they mostly left and we began to grow. If you're going to grow you got to do it the way that Forest Creek Church did."

The advice of Jerry, a new member, was seriously considered. But, as the night wore on, one long-standing member whispered to me after the meeting. "I'm not sure we want to be a copy of Forest Creek Church."

Forest Creek Church was well known in this area. It had been an early adopter of a "seeker-friendly" format on Sunday mornings. The Sunday services are professionally executed, embracing an audience orientation rather than a participatory environment. Quality music, poignant drama, and highly applicable sermons are characteristic of these services. This format is used because services are designed to be "user-friendly" for the nonchurchgoer who is "seeking" a relationship with God. As a result, the seeker-friendly format has been very successful in introducing many non-churched people to Christianity.[5]

"It's clear that we've got a lot to learn," said Leon, another long-standing lay leader. But his openness was merely a gracious facade, as a conversation a few minutes later revealed.

After most people had left, I lingered to talk to Leon. "It sounds like you are open to some of these ideas," I observed. "Not really," Leon replied with candor. "Forest Creek Church isn't doing that good. And we don't need another Forest Creek here in town. Jerry is too used to the way things are run at Forest Creek. The new ideas are not going to work here."

I had heard many good ideas voiced by Jerry that could work remarkably well at this aging church, but I had noticed that Leon and others were less impressed. It now appeared that the overassertive manner in which Jerry had lauded his old church had put off the church leaders.

Trigger 1: The Conflicting Ideas Event

From these examples, we see the workings of Trigger 1, the Conflicting Ideas Event, and the resultant Stage 2 of Idea Development. Now that we've observed this trigger in action, let's define it.

Trigger 1: The Conflicting Ideas Event. Attendees of a church are exposed to an idea-generating event where they pick up new ideas that they feel should be implemented at the church they attend. These ideas conflict with ideas held by the status quo.

This first trigger, the Conflicting Ideas Event, pushes a church out of the "relative harmony" of Stage 1 and into Stage 2, and gives budding change proponents the motivation to seek change.

Conflicting Ideas Events are widespread and are likely to affect all churches at some time. The number of seminars, books, and workshops that propose new and innovative strategies are almost countless.[6] Since idea-generating events are numerous and avoiding them would be fruitless, we must develop a strategy that will allow us to garner appropriate ideas and implement them without causing division.

CHARACTERISTICS OF TRIGGER 1: THE CONFLICTING IDEAS EVENT

Examples of "Trigger 1: Conflicting Ideas Events" include, but are not limited to:
- leadership books
- guest speakers
- magazine articles
- worship seminars
- an evangelistic crusade
- an enthusiastic acquaintance
- private study
- a former church's way of doing things
- a nearby church's way of doing things

Stage 2: Idea Development

How New Ideas Didn't Develop at Hilltop Chapel

After experiencing a Conflicting Ideas Event, change proponents usually become convinced their church needs to change by implementing some of the ideas to which they have been exposed. This change may be in a church's structure, vision, or ministry. Typically, these changes deal with styles of worship, theological issues (spiritual gifts, healing, modes of baptism, etc.), or leadership structure. Change proponents will perceive change as an improvement or modernization, but the status quo will view them as undermining cherished traditions.

I had arrived at this wealthy, and apparently healthy, suburban church named Hilltop Chapel to assist in long-range planning. When a series of focus groups were convened, a rising chorus of concern over the need to change began to take center stage.

"It's just that we're too old to do all of this work. It's time we get some young people in here. If they want to change things, that's fine." The sentiments of this elder statesman were echoed by others in attendance.

"But if we aren't careful," cautioned a female group member, "we'll lose those people again (change proponents) just like we did three years ago." As the story unfolded, she shared her anxiety over the potential repetition of an earlier exit of change proponents. Two days later, I interviewed some of those who had left.

"THEY SAID WE'D BE WELCOME TO BRING SOME CHANGE."

"We tried to work within the system," began a young professional who had left the church in the exit three years ago. "But their actions didn't match their words. They said we'd be welcome to bring some change, and they let us continue until we started talking about worship then everything broke loose." "It came down to them or us," stated a young mother. "They told us 'that's not the way things are done here,' and they're right, it's not."

Though the exit was painful for Hilltop Chapel, there were some positive results. Most of the change proponents found a church home in a nearby congregation of Boomers and Generation X-ers.

Positive results also occurred for Hilltop. The church, even some of the former status quo, realized that change was necessary to keep their ministry relevant to younger generations. This openness was a positive outcome, but this did not mean that the battle for change was over.

"YOU DON'T HAVE TO CONVINCE US, BUT YOU HAVE TO CONVINCE THE AVERAGE PEW-SITTER."

"I don't think you'll have any luck with most people here at Hilltop," stated a member of the status quo. "I don't think the average person at Hilltop understands the changes that are going to be needed. You don't have to convince us, but you have to convince the average pew-sitter."

This senior saint had placed his finger squarely on the pulse of the change process. Some of the status quo among the leadership had recognized the need to accommodate cultural differences of younger generations, but this man was warning there was not the same understanding in the congregation. Simply going through a group exit of change proponents does not mean the status quo are, by and large, ready to embrace or even tolerate change.

Stage 2: Idea Development

Now that we've defined Trigger 1 and described the stage that it produces, let's define the stage that follows, Stage 2: "Idea Development."

Stage 2: Idea Development. New ideas begin to develop within the congregation. A subtle polarization begins to take place, but groups do not yet coalesce. Change proponents patiently hope that others will come to see the wisdom of their new ideas. The status quo may be unaware of these ideas or hoping the change proponents will come to their senses and abandon their new ideas.

Trigger 1, the Conflicting Ideas Event, propels a church out of Stage 1 into this second stage of Idea Development. This stage may be the hardest to detect, but it can also be the most menacing because of its hidden workings.

In Stage 2, new ideas are beginning to gel among the change proponents. When they begin to toss ideas around in conversations, they talk about the general direction of the church rather than particulars. A formal structure does not yet exist in their strategy.

At this stage, change proponents have not yet coalesced into a group. They tend to embrace their ideas as a loose collection of individuals rather than an identifiable faction. During Stage 2, the status quo also exhibit some distinctive behaviors. First and foremost is that many of the status quo are unaware of the growing dissatisfaction of the change proponents. Unfortunately, this lack of knowledge can create greater rifts later. The lack of knowledge occurs in part because change proponents operate in different circles than the status quo.

But even in those scenarios where the development of new ideas is detected, sometimes the status quo will adopt a "they'll come to their senses" attitude. Here, status quo adherents believe that change proponents will see the error of their ways, and embrace the traditional manner of doing things.[7]

Stage 2 Idea Development ensues until Trigger 2 forcefully pushes the church into Stage 3: "Change."

QUESTIONS FOR GROUP STUDY, CHAPTER 6

Are You In (or Headed Into) STAGE 2: Idea Development?

1. Can you recall any idea-generating events that resulted in new ideas being proposed for your church?
   - If so, list the idea-generating events.
   - Make a list of corresponding ideas that came out of each event.
   - Rate the new ideas by the emotional intensity each generated.

2. Do you think the status quo of your congregation understand the ramifications of the changes the change proponents are proposing? If not, what do you foresee as the outcome?

3. In your opinion, do the status quo of your congregation hope that the change proponents will come to their senses and abandon their new ideas? If yes, what is the foreseeable outcome?

CHAPTER 7
Stage 3: Change

He that can have patience can have what he will.
—Benjamin Franklin[1]

Route A or B? Your Two Routes

In the change process, there are two different routes that can be selected at this juncture. One route (I call this Route A) results when Trigger 2 occurs as a Negative Legitimizing Event. In contrast, the other route (I label this Route B) is the direction the change process will take if Trigger 2 is a Positive Legitimizing Event instead.

ROUTE A: WHEN TRIGGER 2 IS A *NEGATIVE* LEGITIMIZING EVENT

If the negative form of Trigger 2 Legitimizing Event occurs, the change process will be pushed down Route A, which eventually leads to group exit. This is described as a negative event because it produces the unintended and negative effect of pushing a group out of the church.

Route A leads to group exit. Route A results when Trigger 2 occurs as a Negative Legitimizing Event. The result of Route A is that a group will eventually exit the church.

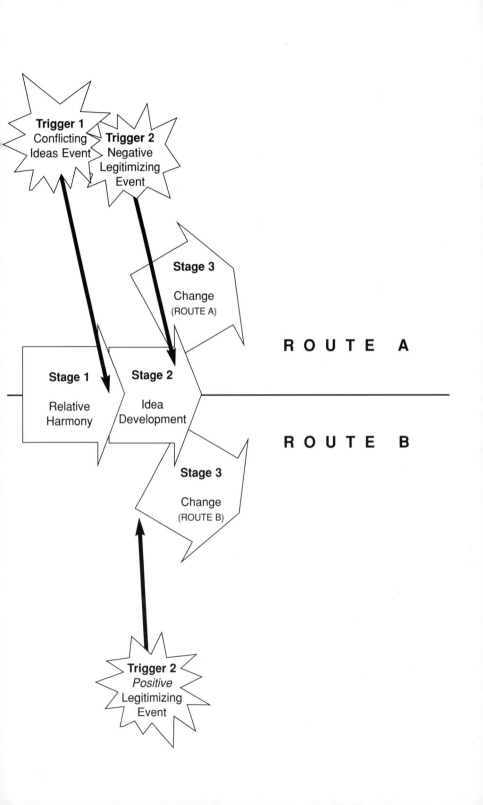

ROUTE B: WHEN TRIGGER 2 IS A POSITIVE LEGITIMIZING EVENT

If the Legitimizing Event occurs in a positive form, then the change process will follow Route B, which eventually results in a group staying with the church. Here is my definition:

Route B leads to group retention. Route B results when Trigger 2 occurs as a Positive Legitimizing Event. The result of Route B is that a group exit is prevented.

The First of Two Critical Triggers That Prevent Group Exit

Trigger 2 is not the only decisive trigger in the change process (Trigger 4 is also highly critical). But Trigger 2 is the first we shall encounter.

Trigger 2: The Negative Legitimizing Event

Route A: Conflict Ahead

RECALLING SOUTHEAST CHURCH, PART 1

Let us recall our story of Southeast Church from chapter 4. If you are using the Quickstart Guide and have skipped chapter 4, it may be helpful to return to that chapter and review it.

Southeast Church had been a prestigious church with more than four hundred attendees in the 1970s. However, by the mid-90s, the church had dropped to less than sixty in regular attendance. As could be expected, the leaders were paralyzed with fear about their future. That is why they jumped at the chance to hire an up-and-coming pastor named Jim.

Jim had been successful at bringing about change during two previous assistant pastorships. However, in both situations, he had been under the tutelage of a mature and diplomatic senior pastor. Jim was highly regarded as a gifted initiator of new programs. Thus, Jim's success at his earlier pastorships made him seem like the ideal candidate for Southeast Church.

YELLOW LIGHTS INSTEAD OF GREEN LIGHTS

The church leaders so wanted to save their aging and dwindling congregation, that they unconsciously gave Jim overly optimistic impressions of their willingness to change. Jim perceived that he had a green light from the leaders of the congregation, when he really only had a yellow light to "proceed with caution."

Now, let's pause for a moment to consider the second of our list of exit antidotes.

Exit Antidote 2: *Leaders may so desperately want to save a dwindling or aging church that they may overstate the status quo's willingness to accept change.* Therefore, if you are attempting to bring change to a congregation that is concerned about future viability, proceed at a pace that is somewhat slower than the status quo is encouraging. Though this restraint may be hard to marshal, it will prevent the onset of polarization.

After returning from the seminar on modern worship, to which Jim invited primarily members of the change proponents, Jim pushed heavily for changes in worship.

Jim soon declared his intentions to begin a modern worship service that summer. New media and sound equipment would need to be purchased and, in his sermon, he thanked the church's leadership for giving him the "green light to go ahead with all of these plans."

The change proponents began to feel bolder in their plans. After all, the status quo had verbally supported Jim's ideas since the day he arrived at Southeast.

However, what Jim and most members of the congregation did not realize, was that Trigger 2 had occurred, and it was already propelling the church down Route A toward division, strife, and eventual group exit.

A Negative Legitimizing Event on Route A
(Conflict and Group Exit Ahead)

Jim's public pronouncements had been a Negative Legitimizing Event. Though no one called it this, his public declarations served to legitimize the changes sought by the change proponents. In addition, Jim's pronouncements legitimized the fears of the status quo that the changes would be too broad and too bold.

A Legitimizing Event is an event or episode where views about change are blessed, championed, or legitimized by an authority figure.

Therefore, Trigger 2 could be defined as the following:

Trigger 2: *A Negative Legitimizing Event* is an event or episode where change proponents' views on change are inadvertently blessed, championed, or legitimized by an authority figure, resulting in polarization between the change proponents and the status quo.

CHARACTERISTICS OF TRIGGER 2: A NEGATIVE LEGITIMIZING EVENT

Characteristics of a Negative Legitimizing Event include, but are not limited to, the following:

- The authority figure does not recognize the implications of his or her statement.
- The result of the negative Legitimizing Event is a widening gulf, sometimes called a fault line, between the change proponents and the status quo.[2]
- The group that is inadvertently blessed or legitimized proceeds quickly with its ideas.
- The group that is not legitimized will often balk at the rapid pace and extensive nature of the ideas of the other group.

At this point, another exit antidote becomes evident.

Exit Antidote 3: *The church leader is expected to keep the "other" side in line.* A pastor or leader who too highly identifies with one party, in lieu of the other, will only further exacerbate the fault lines that can easily become battlelines. Diplomacy dictates the leader be a moderator and facilitator of unity.

The Negative Legitimizing Event propels the church into Stage 3: Change. But before we consider this important stage, let's look at the very different Route B that emerges when Trigger 2 is a Positive Legitimizing Event.

Trigger 2: The Positive Legitimizing Event

Route B: Harmony and Change Ahead

An interim pastor named Dr. Thompson was appointed to shepherd Southeast Church. Nearing retirement, he was the successful pastor of a large, but aging, urban congregation. To me, he did not appear to be a logical choice for an interim leader.

His unhurried and easygoing nature seemed the antithesis of the strong, forward-looking leader that many leadership books extol. Yet, it would turn out that, in this situation, Dr. Thompson's temperament was exactly what the church needed.

Dr. Thompson began his tenure in much the same way as Jim, his predecessor. Dr. Thompson invited a group of leaders to join him at a denominationally sponsored seminar on church growth. However, Dr. Thompson veered from his predecessors' strategy by inviting an equal number of leaders from both the status quo and the change proponents.

After returning from the seminar, tensions over change appeared to be resurfacing again and the congregation braced for more open warfare. Instead, Dr. Thompson asked the leaders to join him in a three-week period of prayer and contemplation regarding the new ideas. Side-by-side, both change proponents and the status quo began to focus on the unifying practices of the church.

Then Dr. Thompson suggested the leaders continue in prayer but also begin informal discussions about the new ideas from the seminar.

After another three weeks had passed, Dr. Thompson suggested that the change proponents present their proposal in written and verbal form to the church council. Since bipartisan dialogue had shaped the ideas that would be presented, the plans had broad support at the council meeting.

Because the change process had been carefully analyzed and discussed, the new ideas included elements that allayed the fears of both groups.

Defining a Positive Legitimizing Event on Route B (Harmony and Change Ahead)

Dr. Thompson's leadership style had drawn the two emerging parties—the status quo and the change proponents—into bipartisan dialogue and eventual harmony.

Part of his unhurried strategy was a six-week Legitimizing Event. Dr. Thompson's actions legitimized the need for change. But, he allowed time for the unifying ministries of the church to take center stage, and for bipartisan concerns to be discussed and addressed.

Since this Legitimizing Event did not polarize factions but, rather, encouraged bipartisan planning and agreement, I have labeled this a Positive Legitimizing Event.

Trigger 2 can be defined in the following manner.

Trigger 2: *A Positive Legitimizing Event* is an event or episode where change proponents' views about change are blessed, championed, or legitimized by an authority figure who does so in an unhurried, prayer-infused, and deliberate manner that not only results in change, but also builds harmony between the change proponents and the status quo.

CHARACTERISTICS OF TRIGGER 2: A POSITIVE LEGITIMIZING EVENT

Characteristics of a Positive Legitimizing Event include, but are not limited to, the following:

- There is an extended time of prayer before strategies are developed. This interval releases the Holy Spirit to foster unity among competing groups.
- The process is unhurried, but deliberate. The leadership neither rushes in to implement new ideas, nor neglects them.
- Neither group was "inadvertently" blessed or legitimized. The legitimization happened through the Holy Spirit (through prayer), interaction (through working together), and eventually through the authority figure's diplomatic and judicious pronouncements.
- The process is transparent. There is no attempt to work behind the back of another group. Both the status quo and the change proponents talk about their ideas in candid and honest discussions.

The Positive Legitimizing Event still propels the church into Stage 3: Change. However, a *Positive Legitimizing Event* will bring change through Route B, instead of the divisive side-taking that characterizes Route A.

Stage 3: Change

How Trigger 2 Propels Us into Stage 3

A Legitimizing Event has a great deal of power. Hasty and partisan legitimization by an authority figure has the potential to propel the change process down Route A and toward group exit. In contrast, unhurried, prayer-infused legitimization by an authority figure can foster harmony and bipartisan support for change. Either way, the authority figure's power to propel the process toward group exit (Route A) or toward group retention (Route B) is profound.

Trigger 2, in both its negative and positive forms, brings about the same initial result: the entering of Stage 3. From the research by Dyck and Starke, it appears that Trigger 2 always pushes a church into at least considering change. What is remarkable from their research is that the manner in which Trigger 2 is employed by an authority figure, either positively or negatively, can be a major step in bringing about group exit or bringing about change.[3]

The power resident in the tongue is aptly described in James 3:5, 6 where the apostle, no stranger to the firestorm that a misspoken word can ignite, compares the influence of a tongue to the power resident in the rudder of a ship or a glowing ember. "Take ships for example," writes James. "Although they are so large and driven by strong winds, they are steered by a very small rudder. . . . Likewise the tongue is a small part of the body, but it makes great boasts. Consider what a great forest is set on fire by a small spark."

The parallel is uncannily illustrative of the power a leader's words have in the change process. Though the biblical admonition is well known, most church leaders have little idea how powerfully their words can bring about change or defeat it. Consequently, if authority figures can suppress their initial enthusiasm for change and allow the congregation to cautiously consider the options, they will ensure that their oral helm does not steer their congregational vessel upon the shoals.

Authority Figures Must Be Careful About What They Say

Because many church leaders are often gifted orators, they tend to be verbally expressive. It is this predilection for self-expression that often gets authority figures in trouble and stymies the change process.

During the change process, verbal expressiveness must be tamed as well as restrained. Pastor Jim's verbal skills, in the example above, were advantageous in his former associate positions. But as a senior pastor, Jim's unbridled declarations exacerbated the problem.

Therefore, a fourth exit antidote might be warranted.

Exit Antidote 4: *Authority figures must be careful about what they say, as well as when they say it.* This is especially true during the change process. Caution, discretion, and judicious behavior are needed to offset hasty implementation of new ideas. Haste usually fosters division.

Conflict Ahead at Elmwood Church

One of the important characteristics of Stage 3 on Route A is that change proponents start to coalesce into an identifiable group within the congregation. This identification may include a name for their group or a regular meeting time or place. At Elmwood Church, it took the form of a Sunday school class.

The young lady was fidgeting as I began a focus group with members of the change proponents at Elmwood Church. She began hesitantly. "We felt more comfortable once we were our own Sunday school class," she said. "It wasn't intentional, but we just wanted a place were we could talk about the Bible and what it had to say about healing." Another group participant chimed in. "We couldn't have talked about it as freely in the Serendipity Class."

The Serendipity Class was a Sunday school class primarily comprised of the status quo. Though several of its participants had actively recruited church newcomers, the mature age of the class had led the newcomers to start their own class. This new class took their name from a passage in the book of Acts that described the harmony of the early church—They called their group "The Acts 2:42 Class" or, simply, "Acts 2:42."

"Acts 2:42 has grown and they (the status quo) don't know how to handle it," continued another focus group participant. "It gives us somewhere in this church where we can talk about the ministry of healing openly and without controversy." Acts 2:42 now numbered more than thirty participants, making it the largest Sunday school class in this congregation averaging 150 in worship attendance.

"We've seen a number of miracles in our class and I know the old timers will be open to it in the church services one day. They haven't seemed threatened by what we're doing, so it's just a matter of time." A few minutes later, another member summed up what many had been alluding to. "Change is going to be easier than any of us thought. They are really behind us." Unfortunately, the difference between expectations and reality was about to set in.

"That's not what that scripture is about!" asserted a member of the Serendipity Class in a different focus group later that day. She was alluding to the name of the new class, Acts 2:42, and the different interpretation she embraced. "Acts 2:42 talks about devoting yourself to the church. It doesn't say to separate yourself and bring up things that don't fit in here. They are mocking the Bible with their name." Other gray heads nodded in affirmation around the room.

The irritation caused by even just the name of this new Sunday class was evident. The change proponents had attempted to select a name that reflected the unity of the early church. Unfortunately, the name had the opposite effect. The new name reflected a growing group identity that coincided with the change proponents coalescing into an identifiable subgroup. The name set this new group apart and, for Serendipity Class members, this only highlighted the emerging fault lines with the Acts 2:42 participants.

Defining Stage 3: Change on Route A (Conflict and Group Exit Ahead)

Now that we have seen some of the inner workings of this stage, let us define Stage 3: Change.

On Route A: Conflict Ahead

Stage 3: Change. This is a period where change proponents begin to coalesce into an identifiable subgroup within the congregation. Early, but limited, success raises the change proponents' expectations that they will be able to implement wide-ranging change.

CHARACTERISTICS OF STAGE 3: CHANGE ON ROUTE A (CONFLICT AHEAD)

Stage 3 is where initial, but limited, success in bringing about change stimulates the change proponents. As a result, change proponents start to implement change outside of their jurisdiction.

For example, bolstered by a sense of widespread support, the Acts 2:42 group began to conduct small healing circles around the sanctuary before the church service.

"It says enter to pray," protested one elder lady and member of the status quo after one service. "That means to be quiet and get your heart right. That doesn't mean to go pushing people over. The laying on of hands is better left for those down the street at the holiness church." But within a moment, her attitude changed and a surprising conciliatory attitude swept over this lady. She concluded with the words, "There's nothing we can do. You can't do without them (the change proponents), so I guess you just let them be."

The introduction of a healing ministry was, in most respects, something that could benefit this stagnant congregation. And there was no particular historical or theological objection to a healing ministry in this denomination.

But it seemed that change was talking place in a way that did not have the appreciation or support of the status quo. It was not an appreciation for God's supernatural power that was the problem, but the haste and lack of bipartisan support with which the practice was implemented. This is a hallmark of Stage 3, for change proponents start to extend change outside of their confines and, in doing this, step on the toes of the status quo.

At this point, however, the status quo does not usually resist the changes, perhaps from the fear of losing the change proponents or because they are largely unaware of the proposed changes.

Characteristics of Stage 3: Change on Route A (Conflict Ahead) include, but are not limited to:

- Change proponents begin to implement changes outside of their confines. This can include:

- using contemporary musical instruments and modern sound equipment in a traditional worship service;
- encouraging the use of new idioms and terminology in worship services (i.e., "unchurched," "dechurched," "cell groups," "believer's baptism," "signs and wonders," and worship "celebration" instead of worship "service");
- encouraging new practices during worship like the lifting of hands, clapping, greeting neighbors in adjacent pews, or including prayer circles.

- The status quo do not actively resist initial changes by the change proponents, either because they seem innocuous, because they are afraid of losing the change proponents, or because the status quo is unaware of the changes.

Route B: Harmony and Change Ahead at Meadowbrook Church

When a positive Legitimizing Event occurs, a congregation begins down the preferred path of Route B. On this route, sides are usually not taken and a church heads toward group retention. A positive Legitimizing Event builds unity and harmony during Stage 3, instead of differences.

Meadowbrook Church sat on a dead end cul-de-sac in a residential neighborhood. Though the church appeared to be hidden from sight for most of the citizenry, the congregation was alive with new families and had just dedicated a new gymnasium. But, at first glance, this congregation had many things going against its growth potential. It was tucked away in an aging residential subdivision. It had very limited parking, and the outside of the building was in disrepair. Yet, within its frail walls was a vibrant and growing church.

The pastor was a man of frail health, seeming to mirror the outward appearance of the church, but he was not frail in spirit. Tom had been shepherd at this church for three years. Upon arrival, he had found himself immersed in the growing tension between the status quo and the change proponents. "They were just about to go at it," he recalled. "I knew from the last church I was at that I better try to do things differently here."

Soon after his arrival, Tom scheduled a retreat, being careful to recruit large numbers of the change proponents *and* the status quo. Before the retreat commenced, Tom met with congregants from both groups in private conversations to present his overview of the situation. "I told all of them that we had to compromise to minister to everyone. It wasn't either this way or that way—we have to have it both ways."

Tom also emphasized the identity of the total church over the identity of any subgroups. Tom later reflected, "I used the model of a family. In it, you've got many different ages and many different ideas. But you are still one entity. You've got to have the same thing in a congregation—one identity but with a lot of different family members."

This high level of compromise behavior set the appropriate tone for the upcoming retreat. In addition, Tom encouraged regular bipartisan prayer groups during the retreat.

At the conclusion of the retreat, the leaders had hammered out innovative ideas that were acceptable to both the change proponents and the status quo. Tom's struggles at an earlier church had led to his success in this setting. Though Tom was not knowledgeable in the workings of the change process, he intuitively understood that compromise and organizational identity must be the hallmark of the process right from the beginning. Sensing emerging fault lines, Tom initiated his own Positive Legitimizing Event in the church retreat.

Defining Stage 3: Change on Route B
(Harmony and Change Ahead)

Now, let us define what Stage 3 looks like when it occurs on Route B, when harmony and change are ahead.

(On Route B: Harmony and Change Ahead)

Stage 3: Change. New ideas are introduced in an unhurried, judicious, and conciliatory way. Prayer accompanies the process, permission is sought, and the identity of the total church is stressed. Consequently, change proponents do not begin to coalesce into a subgroup.

CHARACTERISTICS OF STAGE 3: CHANGE ON ROUTE B
(HARMONY AND CHANGE AHEAD)

Characteristics of Stage 3 on Route B:
• Subgroups do not coalesce.
• Sides are not taken.
• Fault lines, caused by conflicting opinions, do not arise.
• Unity-building exercises, such as working together or retreats, help promote understanding and goodwill along with common goals among the status quo and the change proponents.
• Tolerance is evident among both the status quo and the change proponents.
• Emotional identity is more aligned with the overall organization than with subgroups.

A Caution About Our Infatuation with Newness

As the stories in this and earlier chapters illustrate, new ideas can resonate so robustly with people that old ideas are openly disparaged. In addition, the zeal spawned through an infatuation with newness can readily overpower common sense and unhurried action. Because our love affair with newness and novelty is so pervasive, it becomes essential that any successful strategy approach innovation in an unhurried, cautious and judicious manner.

Therefore, the reader is encouraged to:

• pray diligently before progressing with any new ideas;
• read carefully the information contained within this book (the endnotes provide avenues to more research and related themes);
• share this information broadly, especially with members of both the change proponents and the status quo;
• progress slowly, allowing unity, goal-ownership, and bipartisan support to emerge.

Stage 3: Change

"Where's the Disclaimer?"

"You ought to have a disclaimer!" declared the young lady of about thirty. The scene was very different from the story above, and occurred about six months later in a seminar I conducted on "Why People Leave the Church Over Change." She was the second or third person in the receiving line that evening. At first, I was taken back by the forward tone of her salutation.

"If what you say is right, then you ought to have a disclaimer. All of you." By now all eyes were on this diminutive lady with the lively observation. "You should tell people to take it easy and don't get so worked up over new ideas," she continued. "If they're likely to get all worked up and push too hard for new things, then you ought to warn people. Where's the disclaimer?"

This woman had taken me at my word, and now she admonished me (and other leaders) to include a warning in our seminars that our hearers should implement these new ideas in an unhurried, thoughtful, and conscientious manner.

Her counsel was brash, but her idea was correct.

Let's look at another exit antidote that naturally develops from this understanding.

Exit Antidote 5: *When advocating new ideas, encourage your listeners to be tactful and cautious.* Build caution and diplomacy into seminars, sermons, lectures, and books. Enthusiastic participants may return to their congregations and inadvertently legitimize or too boldly press for the new ideas they have learned.

QUESTIONS FOR GROUP STUDY, CHAPTER 7

Are You In (or Headed Into) STAGE 3: CHANGE?

1. Has an authority figure made some symbolic statement that conferred legitimization upon either change proponents or the status quo?

- If yes, what was the symbolic statement and where was it given?
- Which group benefited from this symbolic statement—the change proponents or the status quo?
- Can you list five results that have occurred, or possibly may occur, due to this event?

2. Have change proponents and/or the status quo begun to coalesce into identifiable subgroups, coming together in Bible study groups, worship teams, ministry groups, prayer clusters, home fellowship groups, etc.?

3. Have subgroups begun to implement changes outside of their confines? Have they started to:
   - move modern musical sound equipment into the sanctuary or altar area?
   - encourage the adoption of new terms in worship services (i.e., "celebration" instead of service, "unchurched," "dechurched," "cell groups," "believer's baptism," etc.)?
   - encourage the adoption of new practices in worship services (i.e., lifting hands, clapping, greeting neighbors in adjacent pews, etc.)?

   List five positive and five negative results from each change.

4. How has talk about change taken place in your church? Which of the following apply?
   - Have discussions about change taken place in an unhurried manner? Why or why not?
   - Have discussions about change been accompanied by a churchwide or leadershipwide call to prayer? Why or why not?
   - Have authority figures patiently waited to voice their position on change until bipartisan dialogue has taken place? Why or why not?
   - Has your leadership encouraged informal dialogue and unity-building exercises between change proponents and the status quo? Why or why not?
   - Have the importance of compromise and conciliation been

adequately stressed among both the status quo and the change proponents? If not, what do you think should happen? How will it be implemented?

5. Has the overall organizational identity of the church been emphasized instead of the individual identity of subgroups? If not, create a vision statement that describes where you, as a group, believe God is calling your church to go in the future.[4]

Then, follow these guidelines.

- Make sure that both change proponents and the status quo give unhindered input into the drafting of these vision statements.

- Once the statements have been created, use both the status quo and the change proponents to publicize them throughout the church and in the community.

- If either group—the change proponents or the status quo—are not willing to promote these statements, reformulate the task force making sure both groups are sufficiently represented.

CHAPTER 8

Stage 4: Resistance

"Criticism . . . makes very little dent upon me, unless I think there is some real justification and something should be done."
—Eleanor Roosevelt, former First Lady[1]

Trigger 3: The Alarm Event

Defining the Alarm Event

In previous chapters, my approach has been to begin with an illustration of a stage or trigger at work, then define the trigger or stage. At this juncture, because an Alarm Event is unavoidable, it will be helpful to first define what that means. Once we understand the definition of an Alarm Event, the basis for its inevitability will become clear.

Trigger 3: The Alarm Event is a wake-up call to the status quo that the change proponents have, in the status quo's minds, gone too far. The status quo then galvanize into a subgroup (on Route A) or cease to exhibit tolerance (Route B).

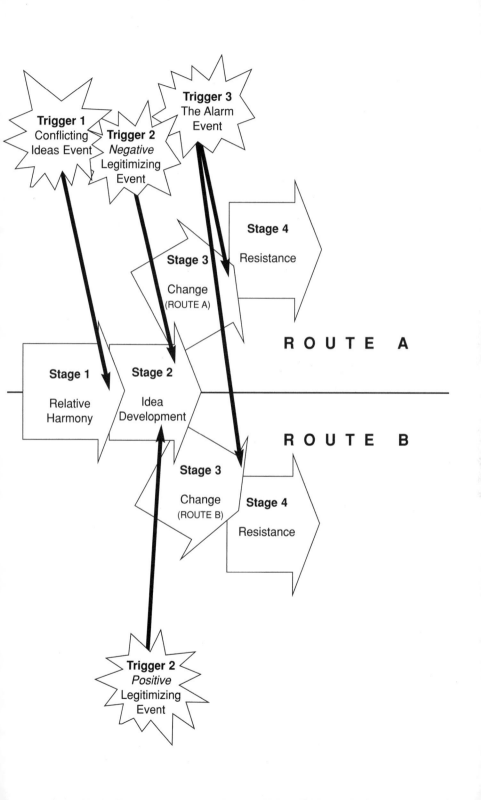

Alarm Events on Route A and Route B

Change means moving from comfortable experiences to more unfamiliar territory. Unfamiliarity, coupled with our human propensity to make mistakes, makes going too far or too fast inevitable. The result is often an Alarm Event.

An Alarm Event is usually encountered regardless of whether a church is headed down Route A (toward conflict and group exit) or Route B (toward harmony and change). Even if a church has successfully begun the change process in a cautious and unhurried manner, an Alarm Event is still on the horizon. Therefore, since the Alarm Event is inescapable it must be planned for in advance.

Alarm Events can also help mediate the process. They keep change proponents from going too far, while helping convince the status quo that change is inevitable. As a result, the Alarm Event can serve as a spark, forcing both the status quo and the change proponents to work together to address the problem. The admonition of Solomon that "as iron sharpens iron, so one man sharpens another" (Proverbs 27:17) reminds us of the biblical notion to let conflict and tension sharpen and further define our ideas.

Yet, in our idealized vision of a church, we wait to see a church at peace, free from conflict-ridden events. Such a church cannot exist in the earthly and fallen realm. Eddie Gibbs argues that such expectations are inconsistent with the church's environment. Gibbs notes that "in mission the church will have to learn to walk by faith, trusting God to be there by his Spirit to guide along the way . . . precisely because the world is in a fallen and broken state, we have to learn to live with diversity, ambiguity and paradox. There is no mission without mess."[2]

Now that we understand that Alarm Events are unavoidable, we will discover that the way the two groups handle them is critical. This is because any existing bipartisan working relationship will now be tested. As a result, churches will discover that all of their ambassadorial and diplomatic skills will be needed to negotiate the unavoidable "mess" of an Alarm Event.

DIFFERENCES IN ALARM EVENTS ON ROUTES A AND B

Route A. After an Alarm Event on Route A (where conflict lies ahead), the status quo begin to form a subgroup, just like the change proponents did after the Legitimizing Event (Trigger 2). Though the status quo possessed some characteristics of a subgroup in the past, they now become a recognizable group, usually distinguished by what they are against.

And this gradual mutation into a subgroup by the status quo becomes noticeable to the change proponents. Change proponents begin to describe the status quo in negative terms such as "those people who don't like contemporary music," "the people who don't believe in healing," or "members who are afraid of new ideas."

Route B. On this route, where a more deliberate, unhurried, and judicious implementation of Stage 3 has resulted in bipartisan support, the status quo do *not* coalesce into a subgroup.

Alarm Events at Water Avenue Church

As I entered the Sunday school wing of Water Avenue Church, the woman made a beeline for me. In her hand, she waved a stack of training materials. Even though it was Sunday morning, and the hall was filling with parents and children heading to Sunday school, Jean began her discourse while still fifteen feet away. And the first words out of her mouth were not reassuring.

"They changed the Sunday school curriculum, and didn't bother to tell me," she explained. "Some of the things Beth wanted to do, I thought were okay. But she didn't ask me about this!"

Beth was the newly elected Christian education chairperson, and had substituted new materials for a curriculum series that had been used in the church for two decades. And, to make matters worse for Jean and others who had become accustomed to the usual curriculum, this new curriculum was not purchased from the denominational publishing house, nor was it a denominationally sanctioned course.

The genesis of this conflict began when Jean, the Christian education chairperson for many years, encouraged a promising newcomer named Beth to take over the position. Now Beth's choice of a popular, contemporary curriculum for Sunday school had robbed Jean of the denominational essence of the curriculum she and others had come to love.

Beth's decision to order new curriculum was not implemented hastily or without forethought. Her decision was the result of her own positive experiences in a Sunday school class. The small group environment of a Sunday school class had provided the intimacy that had bound Beth to other change proponents.

Jean's Sunday school class gave her the same sense of belonging. And, it was in Jean's Sunday school class, populated by members of the status quo, that Jean received some of the greatest outbursts of indignation over the new curriculum.

The dynamics and forces resident in intimate environments, like Sunday school classes, mean that changes in curriculum will strike at the very heart of everyone's church experience. The status quo doesn't want to lose the stability and familiarity of the denominational curriculum, while the change proponents hope to update their experience by adopting newer and more helpful material.

"We've got to have a meeting about this," Jean muttered that Sunday as she walked away. It soon became clear that Beth's decision to change the curriculum had not been brought before the Christian education committee.

Beth approached me after church with her side of the story. She began by acknowledging a mistake had been made. "I didn't mean to make Jean mad, she's been wonderful to me." Beth was almost trembling for she looked up to Jean, and the thought of alienating her mentor was almost too much to bear.

But in the next discourse, the reasons behind Beth's missteps came through clearly. "I thought they had given us permission to make changes. Jean encouraged me to get involved and she liked my ideas. My job as chairperson means I'm supposed to improve things, right? I don't understand why it's such a big thing."

Beth's last phrase sheds some much-needed light on an Alarm

Event. To the change proponent, the Alarm Event does not seem earth shaking in magnitude; it seems like a natural outgrowth or progression in the change process. For the status quo, however, the Alarm Event has crossed a real boundary.

To Jean and other members of the status quo, Beth had gone too far. Change, while initially encouraged by Jean and other status quo members, now hit painfully close to home.

Jean's parting words that Sunday that "we've got to have a meeting about this" had been ominous and signaled that this trigger was now pushing the problem into Stage 4. Days later, the proposed meeting was convened.

Not surprisingly, Beth and the other change proponents did not attend. They weren't told to stay away, but the status quo had conveniently overlooked mentioning the meeting to them. I later asked Jean why she did not invite Beth and she replied, "I didn't think about it at the time, but now I think it might have been because we needed time to lick our wounds."

The change proponents felt that the status quo were coalescing into a definite group. And, the change proponents did not appreciate the clandestine meeting's outcome, for the status quo decided to force through legislation requiring a majority vote of the committee before any change in the curriculum could be inaugurated. Since the status quo retained a majority on the committee, this course of action would be easily attained.

After the next Christian education meeting I was invited to debrief both Jean and Beth in separate interviews. "It felt like I was being punished for trying to improve things," was the way Beth summed up the committee's decision. Jean, on the other hand, summed up the meeting as "a very productive meeting. I really think we defined what we should and shouldn't do at Water Avenue Church."

These are two different perspectives and two different outcomes. As the change proponent, Beth felt like she had been chastised for her well-intentioned actions. Jean and the status quo felt the issue of change was resolved, for they had demonstrated that change would be curtailed if it went too far. Beth, on the other hand, felt the issue was anything but resolved. The tension generated by the Alarm Event would soon thrust both groups into Stage 4: "Resistance."

CHARACTERISTICS OF AN ALARM EVENT (TRIGGER 3)

Let us stop and consider, for a moment, some characteristics of an Alarm Event. Characteristics can include, but are not limited to, the following:

- The change proponents do not see the event as an Alarm Event, but rather as the next logical link in a chain of innovative ideas.
- The status quo:
  - Feel the change proponents have gone too far.
  - Coalesce into a subgroup.
  - Withdraw their initial permission of the change process.
  - Move from tolerance to hindrance.

Exit Antidote 6: *Alarm Events are an unavoidable part of the change process. You cannot avoid them, but you can plan for them.* An Alarm Event is a wake-up call to the status quo that the change proponents have gone too far with some change. This alarms the status quo and they will either galvanize into a faction themselves or, at the very least, cease to exhibit tolerance. Such events are usually an inescapable part of the change process. Expect these skirmishes to arise whenever a change process is initiated. But, if both sides prepare themselves beforehand to work out any problems with conciliation, forgiveness, and in a bipartisan spirit, then the divisive effects of an Alarm Event can be neutralized.

Stage 4: Resistance

How Trigger 3 Propels Us into Stage 4

The atmosphere at Bayview Church had almost taken on the feel of a political caucus. As I entered, I noticed a large banner draped across a foyer wall. "Worship in spirit and truth!" it proclaimed with abstract images of upraised arms. It was Lent, and the congregation was preparing for Easter. However, this and other announcements communicated a feeling that both the change proponents and the status quo were beginning to jockey for dominance of the season.

On an adjacent wall of the foyer, a large poster announced a Maundy Thursday service featuring the choir and selections from J. S. Bach's chorales. In front of the poster sat two choir members who were eager to talk about these upcoming choral events. "We're bringing in a soloist from the city orchestra," stated the man. "I don't think a lot of these young people coming to the church realize how beautiful Bach's music is," declared his wife. "We did it, to a degree, for them."

A few minutes later, I encountered Evan, the pastor and leader of the change proponents at Bayview. After a few pleasantries, the conversation turned somber. Evan told of a council meeting where many of the newer church members, like Evan, had wanted to add modern worship elements to this very liturgical church. The status quo had resisted these changes; modern forms did not blend well with their very formal tradition.

The meeting had gotten a bit out of hand, and two members of the change proponents had quit the board. The disagreement arose because change proponents had already added a ten-minute segment of modern choruses to the beginning of traditional service. The additional choruses took two songs away from the choir and eliminated the organ prelude.

Evan himself announced the changes from the pulpit and they insinuated they would be permanent. With only one very traditional service on Sunday morning, the status quo immediately felt they had lost a significant portion of their liturgical worship expression. The final blow came when a large white projection screen, which was unrolled so that words to the choruses could be displayed, was left unfurled throughout the entire service.

The change proponents had inaugurated these changes without gaining permission from the administrative council and without informing members of the choir. The shock of permanently losing a sizable segment of their traditional worship stunned the status quo.

The change proponents were caught off guard. They felt this alteration of the service was a natural outgrowth of changes they had been suggesting all along. They had even received initial support from the status quo for other, less sweeping changes. This support appeared to give them free rein to implement more change. "Why go through the administrative council or choir?" wondered Evan. "They've been behind us in the past. Who'd think they'd change now?" But this invasion of modern elements into a traditional worship setting had become the Alarm Event that propelled Bayview Church into Stage 4.

As Bayview entered the stage of resistance, less compromise was immediately evident. Each side began informal and formal debates regarding the legitimacy of their views. Both sides called special meetings to discuss the situation. In addition, the change proponents invited a pastor from a smaller, Generation X-orientated church to tell about his success with modern worship. In retaliation, the status quo invited a soloist to demonstrate the beauty of Bach at the Maundy Thursday service.

Soon, as Lent progressed, the church had taken on the look of a political rally, with partisan posters and banners.

Exit Antidote 7: *Discourage the temptation to make middle-of-the-road congregants take sides over change issues.* During Stage 4, factions may attempt to bolster their perspective by recruiting middle-of-the-road people to their cause. However, politicking these noncommitted individuals will polarize a larger portion of the church and eventually make bipartisan plans for change harder to achieve. In addition, because such actions stress group identity over overall church identity, the conscripting of these congregants will work against unity. Such enlistment is unfair to the middle-of-the-road congregants who, due to personal needs, may need to circumnavigate skirmishes.

Stage 4: Resistance on Route B (Change and Harmony Ahead)

EIGHTEEN MONTHS LATER AT WATER AVENUE CHURCH

The reader may remember Jean's last ominous words: "We've got to have a meeting about this." Do you remember the outcome of that meeting? Beth, the change proponent, was informally chastised when the Christian education committee voted to require a majority vote for any change in curriculum. Beth seemed to feel a sense of failure and public humiliation. Beth and her family soon left the church, which caused deep pain for Jean. Both Beth and Jean had been casualties of the process.

Eighteen months later, the church braced for another round of dissension. A new pastor had been appointed. This new shepherd took stock of the pain the church had been through and delicately guided the church toward change. Being careful not to inadvertently legitimize the ideas of the change proponents, the new pastor worked in a more deliberate, unhurried, transparent, and cautious manner. Helen, the new pastor, moved down the more preferred Route B toward change and harmony. In fact, when some of the remaining change proponents at Water Avenue Church resurrected the issue of changing the Sunday school curriculum, the new pastor tactfully moved to address the issue. This time, Jean reacted differently.

Helen did several things that are characteristic of churches on the preferred Route B. Helen encouraged the Christian education committee to solicit curriculum samples from many of the large Christian publishing houses, along with the latest in denominational curriculum. Helen then encouraged the committee to sift through the reams of material. She also asked the committee to put together "opinion groups," of different ages. One group was made up of Builders. Another of Boomers, and a third opinion group was made up of Generation X. The three generations mulled over the mounds of information and picked two curriculums that each felt would be best for congregants of their age. The committee then reconvened to look at the recommendations. Because I was interested in the dynamics involved, I attended the meeting. As I sat there that night, I wondered how different this meeting must have been from that meeting eighteen months before, where Beth had decided to leave. Jean was still in charge, but she had adopted a more conciliatory and unifying position. "I think we have many good lessons here to choose from. I didn't realize how good some of these were." As members around the room added their opinions, there was a growing consensus that maybe two or more curriculums could be used at the same time, with a different curriculum for each age group. "That's never been tried here," was the all-too-expected summation by one group member. Jean countered, "I think if we keep what the Crossroads Class (the status quo Sunday school) wants, then we can also give the other classes something they will like."

Jean had grasped an important concept. The curriculum does not have to be one broad curriculum for all ages. Though this was uncustomary in the church, all finally agreed that, to avoid offending people, multiple curriculums would be in order.

In this journey through Stage 4, some eighteen months after the first crossing of these uncharted waters, Water Avenue Church successfully navigated around disaster. Perhaps it was their first failure with Beth, or perhaps it was the unhurried and cautious mentorship of Helen the new pastor, but now the church emerged from Stage 4 diversified, but moderately unified!

Defining Stage 4: Resistance on Routes A and B

Now that we have these two illustrations in mind, it is time to define Stage 4: "Resistance." Remember, Stage 4 has two manifestations: one on Route A, where conflict is ahead and another on Route B, which results in change and harmony.

Stage 4: Resistance. The status quo see the organization as facing a crisis and seek to keep the change proponents in check. Conversely, the change proponents see the organization as facing an opportunity. Spirited discussions take place, special meetings are held, and votes are taken.

Unique to Route A: (Conflict Ahead): On this route each side argues for the legitimacy of their views and sides are expected to be taken. But, these tensions only stir up more emotions. Though meetings are called, there is little switching of sides. Both sides are aware they are frustrating the goals of the other.

Unique to Route B: (Harmony and Change Ahead): Here there is a high degree of compromise, concession, and conciliation resulting in multifaceted plans that meet the needs of both groups. As a result, both sides work out their conflicts.

CHARACTERISTICS OF STAGE 4 ON ROUTES A AND B

On Route A (conflict ahead) *both the change proponents and the status quo:*
- Are less likely to compromise.
- Argue for the legitimacy of their views.
- Present resolutions to be voted upon.
- Invite outside speakers to support their views.
- Distribute literature supporting their views.
- Politic middle-of-the-road members to join their side.
- Call meetings where there is little switching of sides.

On Route B (change and harmony ahead) *both the change proponents and the status quo:*
- Are more likely to compromise;
- Act in an unhurried, cautious, and ambassadorial manner;
- Are aware they are frustrating each other's goals;
- Call meetings where there is a high degree of effort to compromise and resolve conflict;
- Conduct surveys, focus groups and investigations to discover mutually acceptable plans.

What to Do If You Are in Stage 4: Resistance

If You Are on Route A: Conflict Ahead

As we have seen in Stage 4, the status quo see the organization as facing a crisis and thus seek to keep the change proponents in check, while the change proponents see the organization as facing an opportunity. As a result, each side argues for the legitimacy of their views, inflaming each other emotionally.

If your church is experiencing these signs, indicating you are headed down Route A toward conflict, it is important you do two things:

1. Reacquaint yourself with the characteristics of Stage 2: "Idea Development" (see chapter 6).
2. Return to Trigger 2 and reengineer a Positive Legitimizing Event. See chapter 7 to refresh your memory about characteristics that will create a Positive Legitimizing Event.

By stressing the workings of the total organization, finding common ground and shared beliefs between the two groups, and doing all of this in an unhurried manner, you can incubate a spirit of harmony and conciliation.

EXIT ANTIDOTE 8

Remember, during Stage 2 on the Route toward conflict, we saw that even as polarization increases, groups do not yet coalesce. This last feature is especially important to understand. If you thwart the growth of polarized groups during Stage 2, and follow this with a Positive Legitimizing Event, a church can change from Route A (conflict ahead) to Route B (harmony and change ahead).

Therefore, if you are in Stage 4 and you want to change from Route A to Route B, employ Exit Antidote 8.

Exit Antidote 8: *Learn how to re-legitimize the change process.*
If your church is starting to experience a polarization between change proponents and the status quo, do three things:

1. Identify the Legitimizing Event (Trigger 2) that began the polarization process.
2. Re-legitimize the process by going back and creating a new Legitimizing Event. At this point, it will be helpful to return to chapter 7 to see how to create a Positive Legitimizing Event that occurs in a more deliberate, permission-seeking, cautious, and prudent way.
3. Next, read (or reread if you are not on the Quickstart plan) the portions of chapters 7 and 8 that describe how Stages 3 and 4 occur on Route B, where change and harmony are ahead. Use the insights and the Exit Antidotes from these chapters to reposition your church on Route B.

IF YOU ARE ON ROUTE B: HARMONY AND CHANGE AHEAD

Route B, as you may remember, is characterized by a high degree of compromise, concession, and conciliation; resulting in multifaceted plans that meet the needs of both change proponents and the status quo. Thus, both sides begin to work out their conflicts.

If this describes you, and you are headed down Route B toward harmony and change (or have just made adjustments to go down this route), proceed to the next chapter.

However, even though you have successfully navigated the process of change so far, do not be overconfident. You must now navigate Stage 5, which can be either a period of "intense conflict" or, at the very best, a period of "dissonant harmony." In fact, this next stage and the triggers that inaugurate it may very well be the supreme test of your strategic leadership skills.

QUESTIONS FOR GROUP STUDY, CHAPTER 8

Are You In (or Headed Into) STAGE 4: Resistance?

1. Has an Alarm Event occurred with one or more of the following characteristics?

- The status quo felt that change has come too fast. If this is the case, describe what the status quo reacted to and what timetable they wished had been enacted.
- An event occurred that resulted in the status quo feeling the change proponents had crossed the line. What was the event? Describe the line that was crossed.
- Has the status quo withdrawn some of their support for the change proponents' ideas? If yes, divide a piece of paper into two columns. Write down phrases that describe how the status quo supported change before the Alarm Event on the left. On the right, describe how the status quo's actions changed after the Alarm Event.

2. If an Alarm Event has occurred, are the change proponents aware of how it has affected the status quo? Describe the Alarm Event in two ways. First, write a paragraph describing the Alarm Event from the perspective of a change proponent. Next, write a paragraph describing the Alarm Event from the perspective of the status quo. Compare these two reactions. Ask yourself three questions:
   - What does this tell you about each side?
   - What do you think is ahead if these two viewpoints are left unadressed?
   - Do you see any areas of agreement?

3. Have either change proponents or the status quo called special meetings? If they did, was there any switching of sides? If there was none, you may be on Route A heading toward conflict. However, if there was a degree of resolution, you may be on Route B, a route toward eventual harmony and change. Which route do you think you are on?

4. From your answers to the above questions, do you think you are on Route A headed toward conflict? If you are, return to the subsection of this chapter titled "What Do You Do If You Are in Stage 4: Resistance" and follow the suggestions given there to re-legitimize the process by going back and creating a new Legitimizing Event.

CHAPTER 9

Stage 5 (On Route A): Intense Conflict

The ultimate measure of a man is not where he stands in moments of comfort and convenience, but where he stands at times of challenge and controversy.
—Martin Luther King Jr., civil rights leader[1]

An Introduction to Chapters 9 and 10

Up to this point, I have dedicated a chapter to each of the four stages we have encountered in the exit process. However, the intensity of the emotions generated in Stage 5, along with its two expressions, necessitates the use of two chapters.

In this chapter, let us begin with a description of how Stage 5 occurs on Route A. On this route, the reader will discover that intense conflict usually erupts. Then, in chapter 10, we will examine how Stage 5 occurs when a church is on Route B headed toward harmony and change.

Trigger 4: The Polarizing Event on Route A (Conflict Ahead)

A Short Career at Third Church

Bill was one of the most promising candidates for the pastorate at Third Church. While attending a denominationally affiliated

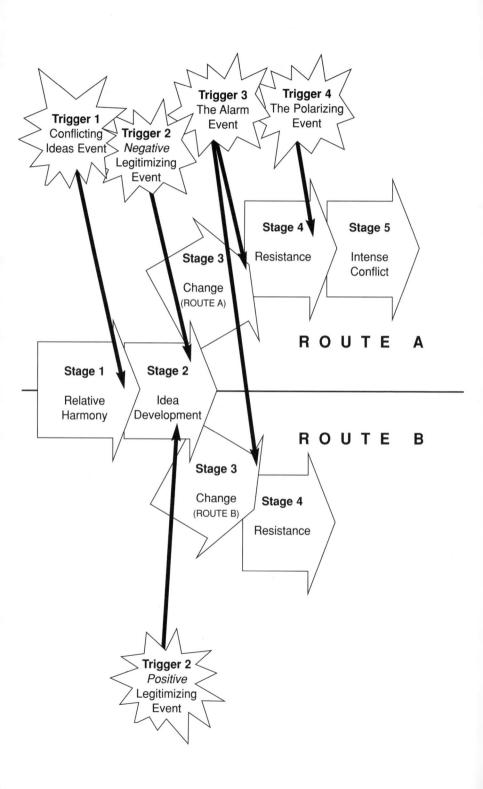

college and seminary, he distinguished himself as the initiator of several new campus ministries.

At the same time, Third Church was emerging as a church with a great deal of potential. It was located on the edge of a moderately sized town of fifty thousand inhabitants, and only twenty-two miles away from a larger city of 200,000. The church averaged only 125 on Sunday mornings, but its location meant it was poised to attract some of the many new residents who were moving to the community.

The potential of this area did not go unnoticed by the business community. A new shopping center had been built nearby, and the creation of an access road now made Third Church highly visible. The result was that Third Church was having an influx of young visitors with new families and new ideas.

To the leaders of Third Church, this looked like the ideal time to change pastors. The current pastor, John, had been at Third Church for fifteen years and often mentioned that he was looking forward to retirement. The church leaders had clandestinely met with the pastor and suggested that, if Bill was available upon his graduation from seminary, it might be time for John to retire.

A slight, but steady, influx of change proponents had alerted the church's leadership that some alterations were needed if they wanted to reach out and retain the younger community residents. After a few setbacks, the leaders at Third Church were successful in securing Bill for the pulpit at Third Church. "Looks like a good fit," John stated to me shortly after Bill was confirmed as the new pastor. But Bill did not turn out to be the shepherd the leaders had in mind, and the church did not turn out to be the congregation Bill expected.

"This Meeting Is Going to Make or Break this Church."

It was two years to the month since Bill had come to Third Church. I received the phone call while on another consulting trip in a nearby state. "This meeting is going to make or break this church," said Bill. "At this meeting I'm going to let them know where I stand. What they want to do will kill the church. The future is these young families. I must take a stand."

Bill had come to the church two years earlier with a bundle of new ideas gleaned from the creative cauldrons of college and seminary. Since John, the former pastor, had given Bill the distinct impression that the church was amendable to new ideas, Bill had hit the floor running. Unfortunately, from the actions that occurred in his first two years, it was apparent that the change process was on Route A, where conflict was ahead.

Let's now take a brief look at how Third Church encountered each trigger and stage in the change process on Route A.

Stage 1: Relative Harmony. Prior to a surge in population in the surrounding area, the members of Third Church were relatively satisfied with the church's purpose and how it was being carried out in the community.

Trigger 1: Conflicting Ideas Event. Young families began moving into the area and started attending Third Church. Initially, longtime members were enthusiastic about this youthful influx. However, many of these newer members brought a preference for the modern worship they had enjoyed in other congregations.

Stage 2: Idea Development. At first, the status quo expressed immense delight with these new arrivals, and solicited ideas from them that might reach their young friends. As the newcomers proposed changes in worship styles that they felt would attract their youthful acquaintances, they started to develop into change proponents.

Trigger 2: Legitimizing Event. Not long after arriving at Third Church, Bill publicly supported the newer members who wanted to add a modern worship service. He preached several sermons on the legitimacy of modern worship. His actions became a Legitimizing Event that emboldened the change proponents and thrust the church into Stage 3.

Stage 3: Change. The change proponents began to make changes in the sanctuary to accommodate a newly added modern worship service. The status quo still had their traditional worship at 10:45 A.M., but now it was preceded by a modern service at 8:00 A.M. The change proponents scattered modern musical instruments and amplification across the pulpit area, and erected a large projection screen. Due to the extensive nature of these changes, it was not possible to remove them before the traditional worship service. As a result, the status quo now had to bear the intrusion of these hi-tech elements into their traditional service. Though the status quo complained, the change proponents felt they would eventually win them over. Sides were not yet taken, but fault lines between the groups were beginning to emerge.

Trigger 3: Alarm Event. The change proponents pushed a motion through the administrative council to switch the service times. The younger families that attended the modern service had young children to get to church, and lobbied for the modern service to be moved to a more convenient 10:45 A.M. and the traditional service moved to 8 A.M. The change proponents did not see this as an Alarm Event; for them it was only a natural progression in the change process. But to the status quo, this was definitely an Alarm Event. The status quo did not like how the change proponents had garnered an upper hand (not to mention a majority) on the administrative council. In addition, the administrative council had circumvented the worship committee in which the status quo still retained a majority. It was not just the moving of the traditional service that alarmed the status quo, it was the newfound influence and power of the change proponents.

Stage 4: Resistance. The change proponents thought that the status quo only needed to be educated on the subject. They invited them to attend a seminar in the nearby city on modern worship. No members of the status quo participated. In response, the status quo called several extra meetings of the worship committee, where they still retained a majority, and invited members of the administrative council to attend. Though there was a great exchange of ideas, there was no switching of sides.

As a result, the church was poised at the doorstep of Stage 5: "Intense Conflict." All the church needed was a Polarizing Event (Trigger 4) to thrust it into this next stage. And Bill had unknowingly provided the venue.

Exit Antidote 9: *Don't think the solution is just to educate the other side.* Both change proponents and the status quo must be careful not to assume that the other side simply needs to be educated for them to change their opinions. Oftentimes seminars, workshops, books, and videos are seen as tools to re-educate a faction that is hesitant. Actually, what is lacking is not instruction, but preparation for the acceptance of new ideas. Therefore, do not count on training tools as the remedy but, rather, foster dialogue, compromise, and patience, allowing bipartisan solutions on change to emerge.

Bill had called for a meeting of the administrative council to address the issues that the worship committee had been unable to defuse. Knowing the administrative council had a majority of change proponents, Bill expected to lay the issue to rest once and for all.

Bill had always felt that he had been hired to bring about change, and what he perceived as desperate requests from the church led him to believe that almost any new ideas would be acceptable. However, once the status quo had seen the extent and the rapidity of the change embraced by the change proponents, they became alarmed (Trigger 3) and developed greater resistance (Stage 4). As a result, they now looked to Bill to keep these new ideas from dividing Third Church.

The council meeting seemed like an ambush to Bill. Attendees included almost two dozen older members, most of whom had been on the administrative council in the past. Though no longer members of the council, they now attended as "concerned" parties.

As the conversations began and the exchanges heated in intensity, it became clear to Bill this was not the meeting he had in mind. Nevertheless, he rose to his feet and made a bold and unwavering declaration of support for the change proponents. His pronouncement was intended to unequivocally state the direction in which the church would head and quell growing dissent. Rather than quell the tension, Bill's remark gave the status quo a new target.

The status quo felt that it was Bill's job to bring about change that was in keeping with their traditional way of doing things. They wanted change that didn't hurt. While this is probably an unreasonable (and unobtainable) proposition, the status quo were right in expecting Bill to lead the church in a harmonious journey toward change. In the minds of the status quo, Bill had failed at keeping the change proponents and the status quo on the same team. Now Bill was seen as part of the problem.

Frank, a gentleman with a long family history in the church, stood up to address the meeting. Though he was known as a vocal spokesperson of the status quo, he had been largely silent to this point. Now, as he prepared to break his uncharacteristic silence, all eyes were upon him. "I think Bill is not part of the solution, but part of the problem," Frank said. "I've prayed a great deal about this and I feel it's either time for my wife Barbara and I to go, or for him to go."

The change proponents were stunned, none more so than Bill. He had always known success throughout his college and seminary career. Bill had never felt such a sense of failure and disappointment as he did at that moment. This overwhelming feeling of disenchantment and frustration led to his next action.

Exit Antidote 11: *Watch out for the sucker punch.* This is a situation where an antagonist, either consciously or unconsciously, tries to elicit a passionate and imprudent response from a leader. A leader who "resigns in protest" is one example of such a response. Such actions produce guilt that will further estrange factions. Therefore, leaders must come to potentially divisive meetings with their emotional energies under control. Do not let passions erupt into poor decisions. Check your emotions at the door, or don't go.

Let's return to our list of triggers and stages. We last described Third Church in Stage 4: Resistance. Now let us recap the event that took place at the council meeting called by Bill.

Trigger 4: Polarizing Event. The council meeting became a Polarizing Event for the church. The status quo immediately began to entertain the idea that pastoral leadership could be at fault for not guiding the change process in a more harmonious manner. The change proponents reeled at the idea of losing their champion. Both sides began to intensify the conflict, as the focus moved away from worship styles and toward Bill.

After three hours, Bill had had enough. His ego and pride had certainly been hurt, but those feelings were superseded by the prospect of a church separating over his leadership. In a convulsion of frustration and despair Bill stood and declared, "I resign from this church effective Monday. I didn't come to tear this church apart." Everyone in attendance was stunned; even Frank had not intended or expected such an immediate response.

That Sunday was Bill's last sermon from Third Church's pulpit. It was remarkably free of criticisms. As I sat there, I was proud of Bill's control and restraint. But as Bill concluded, he succumbed to one subtle, but disparaging, remark. Bill stated, "After tomorrow I am no longer your pastor. You must put everything behind you and forget about what I've been through. You will have a very capable pastor soon, and you must give him your loyalty and support." I noticed tears being brushed from eyes across the auditorium. Rather than healing the rift, Bill's parting words seemed to say "please forget about me." This further exacerbated the problem. Lyle Schaller correctly calls such comments "means of inducing guilt."[2] As such, Bill's parting words had subtly fostered guilt in the change proponents for not standing more forcefully with him, and in the status quo for casting blame in his direction.

Defining the Polarizing Event (Trigger 4)

THE FOUR P'S

The above is just one example of a how a Polarizing Event might occur, for a Polarizing Event may take many forms. However, there are some common distinctives. The four characteristics of a Polarizing Event (I have labeled them the four P's) are listed in the following definition of this trigger event.

On Route A: Conflict Ahead

Trigger 4: The Polarizing Event is an event, usually **public,** that causes both the status quo and the change proponents to feel they have received a **personal** attack and been unfairly treated. It transforms the **point of focus** of the conflict from specific actions to general attitudes, and results in uncompromising polarization on both sides that could have a **permanent** effect. This event may be characterized by personal criticisms, inflexible positions, public condemnation, pastoral resignation or removal, and/or binding votes limiting the influence of certain groups.

CHARACTERISTICS OF A POLARIZING EVENT (TRIGGER 4)

Some general characteristics that often accompany a Polarizing Event include, but are not limited to:

- *Public criticism:*
  Public meetings are called:

♦ To "rectify" the situation.
♦ Where both sides as well as nonpolarized members witness the fray.

Public pronouncements are given:
♦ A leader unwaveringly and publicly supports action by either the status quo or the change proponents.
♦ A leader explicitly and publicly criticizes action by either the status quo or the change proponents.

• *Public criticism:*
Personal attacks:
♦ Individuals are publicly accused of unacceptable behavior.
♦ Commitment to the denomination, the church, or God is questioned.

• *Unfair treatment:*
♦ Actions are taken without the approval of those they affect.
♦ Authority is circumvented or disregarded.

• *Point of focus changes:*
From specific strategies, such as:
♦ Worship styles or practices.
♦ Christian education format or curriculum.
♦ Outreach methods.

To the general philosophy or overall attitude of the church and/or leaders, and their commitment to:
♦ Reach the lost.
♦ Open up its leadership positions to newer attendees.

• *Permanent solutions result:*
Votes are taken:
♦ To limit the influence of the status quo or the change proponents.
♦ To remove a pastor or other leader.

Resignations take place.
♦ Church members or board members resign.
♦ Pastors or paid staff resign.

Stage 5 (On Route A): Intense Conflict

As you can see, a polarizing event has many personal, public, and permanent ramifications. In fact, due to their high profile and scandalous nature, these events often color the perspective of potential attendees outside of the church. The outreach potential of a church suffers greatly after such events.

Two Crucial Triggers: Trigger 2, and Now Trigger 4

Earlier in this book, I mentioned that, if Trigger 2 could be changed from a negative Legitimizing Event to a positive Legitimizing Event, conflict could be avoided. Next we will see that if Trigger 4's Polarizing Event is changed into a Harmonizing Event, group exit can usually be prevented. These are the two crucial triggers that must be changed if group exit is to be avoided.

However, before we discuss how to create a positive Harmonizing Event in chapter 10, let's look at how Intense Conflict (Stage 5) develops after a Polarizing Event.

Stage 5: Intense Conflict

On Route A (Conflict Ahead)

HOW A POLARIZING EVENT PROPELS US INTO STAGE 5

As we noted, Trigger 4 will push a church toward a clash of passions. The Polarizing Event accomplishes just what its name suggests—it thrusts the change proponents and the status quo into side-taking and conflict. Each group is less likely to compromise, and begins moving toward entrenchment. And, in the minds of both sides, such actions are the product of acting upon principle. At Third Church, the change proponents soon sought avenues to show their loyalty to their departed pastor and hold unwaveringly to his ideas on change. Their champion had fallen but their battle cry would be louder than ever.

The status quo saw Bill's hasty resignation as proof of his shortcomings. In their minds, Bill had let his passions and preferences take precedence over his duties and obligations. They expected him to share their vulnerabilities, their worries, and their discomfort.

Subsequently, both sides began to dig in. Entrenchment ensued. Concession and negotiation were over. Now fault lines erupted into battle lines.

Stage 5: Intense Conflict at Third Church

Let's return to the scene after the meeting at Third Church where Bill resigned as pastor.

For the status quo, Bill's abrupt resignation confirmed that Bill was not the shepherd for them. To many, Bill's actions at the meeting were glaring examples of his lack of skill in mediation. Frank's declaration that "Bill is not part of the solution, but part of the problem" summed up the perceptions of the status quo. What the status quo failed to anticipate was how deeply Bill's supporters would empathize with their fallen leader.

The change proponents had looked upon Bill as an extension of themselves. If the status quo could do this to Bill, they would eventually do it to them. Bill's resignation served as an unconscious model for change proponents to consider.

Exit Antidote 12: *You are not necessarily next in line to get mistreated.* Simply because someone has been mistreated during the change process (fired, asked to leave, forced to resign, or otherwise ill-treated) does not mean you are next. Oftentimes, those behind such mistreatment will sense the unjust nature of their action and be less likely to repeat it in the near future. Therefore, if ill treatment has recently taken place, an opportunity for concession and conciliation may be at hand.[3]

Regrettably, this opportunity for conciliation was overlooked at Third Church. Within two months five change proponents on the administrative council had resigned, turning the balance of power back to the status quo.

Not surprisingly, the status quo restored the original times for the worship services. Since the change proponents felt their needs and preferences were neglected, attendance at the modern service dropped off markedly.

At first, it was just a few unsigned letters to the administrative council, criticizing the restoration of the service times. But these letters carried an ominous tone, with one letter alluding to the fact that "there are people who are ready to leave the church." These threatening letters only solidified the perception of the status quo that the change proponents, who insinuated in their letters that the status quo were destroying the church, should be the ones to leave.

Though change proponents on the council had begun leaving the church, other change proponents, those average laypersons who had not been in key leadership positions, held out hope that change might still be pushed through. It was these rank-and-file members of the change proponents who began escalating the fray. They soon convened by-invitation-only meetings to discuss what was happening. And they began to publicly criticize the status quo's leadership.

"WE ENCOURAGE THOSE PEOPLE WHO CANNOT FIT IN HERE
TO LOOK ELSEWHERE FOR A CHURCH."

As a result, the administrative council, once again the bastion of the status quo, adopted a motion that people who were dissatisfied at Third Church should consider another church. A short paragraph was issued after one administrative council meeting that read, in part, "recognizing that we are not the only member of the Body of Christ we encourage those people who cannot fit in here to look elsewhere for a church having our support and respect in actions they choose."

Both sides now began to see the exit of the other as a viable alternative to continued bickering. For both groups, the very survival of their church, and perhaps even their spirituality, made it necessary for the other group to leave. Trying to force each other out, the conflict became personalized.

The administrative council meeting held the following month was well attended by both sides. Though many change proponents had resigned from the council, other change proponents attended hoping to accomplish what their colleagues had been unable to do. The change proponents asked permission to air their grievances to the council. The council leadership declared they would take up such matters under "new business" toward the end of the meeting. Thinking their opportunity would occur shortly, the change proponents sat quietly to await their turn.

After several hours, the change proponents began to feel that the status quo members of the council were stalling. The mundane talk of furnace repair and winter snow removal had seemed to trivialize their impending concerns. After several hours the change proponents were ready to burst. And burst they did.

"This is a disgrace," exclaimed one young mother. "The church is dying, and all you care about are roofs and parking lots." Scattered applause followed from the change proponents. The status quo felt rebuffed by the outburst. Soon, one council member retaliated with the statement that "This is the problem. You don't know the right way to do things in a church." The charge that they respected neither proper procedure nor tradition was like waving a red cape in front of the change proponents. This was the problem with the status quo, in their mind—they had more concern for procedure and tradition than for spiritual vibrancy and growth. The intensity of the meeting escalated.

Personal remarks had been off-limits before; now, in Stage 5, Intense Conflict, they were widespread. Competence in leadership styles, degree of financial support, and even Christian commitment were contested that night and on ensuing occasions. Personal affronts, similar to those Bill had experienced, further estranged each side in the growing debacle.

Attendance at the modern worship service soon declined. Within four months, the modern service had ended and the church returned to a state that nearly mirrored its situation prior to Bill's arrival.

A RECAP OF STAGE 5 AT THIRD CHURCH

Now let us recap what was taking place at Third Church by adding Stage 5 to our record of Third Church's progress on the triggers and stages chart.

Stage 5: Intense Conflict. Both sides began to dig in at Third Church. For the status quo, Bill's abrupt resignation confirmed that Bill was not the right shepherd for the job. They saw Bill as unable to diffuse the situation with Frank and this, in their minds, was indicative of his lack of diplomacy. What the status quo failed to anticipate was how personal and public the attack had seemed to Bill and how deeply wounded his supporters would be. Change proponents felt Bill had been pushed out by Frank's ultimatum. They worried that, if the status quo could do this to Bill, it could eventually do this to the other change proponents. As a result, both sides begin to entertain the idea that a group exit might be necessary to preserve their church and their spirituality. As leaders among the change proponents resigned their positions and begin to exit the congregation, rank-and-file change proponents took up the cause, hoping one last push might bring about change.

Defining Stage 5: Intense Conflict
on Route A (Conflict and Group Exit Ahead)

Let's define Stage 5 in the following way:

Stage 5: Intense Conflict is characterized by entrenchment and faultfinding. Each side refuses to compromise or concede for fear of losing ground. Emotional outbursts (publicly, privately, and in written form) question the competence of the leadership, while ultimatums taunt the other group to leave. Fault lines have now become battle lines.

CHARACTERISTICS OF A STAGE 5: INTENSE CONFLICT ON ROUTE A
(CONFLICT AHEAD)

Stage 5, Intense Conflict can occur in many forms, such as:

• Entrenchment:
Invitation-only meetings are held to plan strategies.
There is an absence of concession and compromise as each side now refuses to give in to the other.

• Faultfinding:
Emotional blaming occurs publicly, privately, and in written form.
Members are personally criticized regarding their leadership competence, commitment to the church, and even Christian faithfulness.

• Polarization:
Meetings are called where emotional outbursts characterize the exchange. People may walk out of these meetings in protest.
Denominational leaders are brought in to exhort one side or the other to change their perspective.

A Word About Routes A and B

Route A at Third Church

The last stage is almost upon us. In chapter 11, you will see how a Justifying Event (Trigger 5) pushed the change proponents at Third Church into leaving the congregation. In this upcoming chapter, we will witness Third Church continue down its painful trek on Route A, with conflict ahead.

Route B: The Preferred Choice

Before we consider this disappointing outcome, let us look at what can happen if a church travels Route B, where harmony and change lie ahead. In the next chapter, the reader will discover that, on Route B, both Trigger 4 and Stage 5 can take on very different forms when a church handles the change process judiciously and correctly.

QUESTIONS FOR GROUP STUDY, CHAPTER 9

Are You In (or Headed Into)

Stage 5: Intense Conflict (on Route A)?
  1. Has a Polarizing Event occurred with one or more of the following characteristics:
     • *Personal criticism.* Have individuals been publicly accused of unacceptable behavior? Make a list with two columns. In column 1, list the accusations; in column 2, list the perceived motivations behind the accused person. Ask yourself, do the accusations accurately portray the person's motivations?
     • *Public criticism.* If you have encountered any of these following characteristics, what was the outcome? And what was the expectation?
       • Have public meetings been called to rectify, debate, or solve the situation?
       • Have unexpected members showed up at gatherings ready to air grievances? What was the outcome? What was the expectation?
       • Has a leader publicly supported action by either group or criticized either the status quo or the change proponents?
     • *Point of focus has changed.* Has the point of focus changed from specific actions (such as worship styles, outreach methods, denominational and traditional beliefs, etc.) to the general philosophy or overall attitude of the church and its leaders (such as a commitment to reaching the lost, etc.)?
       • What has been the result of this refocusing on general attitudes rather than specifics?
       • Has this brought the church closer together or farther apart?
       • Make two lists. In list 1, list points of disagreement between the change proponents and the status quo. In list 2, list points of agreement between the change proponents and the status quo. Which list is longer? Which list is more important?

- *Permanent solutions resulted.* Have any of the following occurred?
  - Have votes been taken to permanently institute change, restore the former way of doing things, or limit the influence of the status quo or the change proponents?
  - Have resignations taken place? By whom and for what reasons?
  - What has been the overall result of these permanent solutions? Have they brought the church together or further divided it? What do you wish had been done instead?

2. Has Intense Conflict erupted in your church with some of the following elements?
- *Entrenchment*
  - Are invitation-only meetings held to plan strategies?
  - Do uninvited members attend meetings, perhaps applauding those with their view and deriding those holding opposite viewpoints?
  - Have ultimatums been given that:
    Taunt the other side to find a different church if this one is not meeting their needs?
    Urge the other side to get on board, or get off the ship?
- *Faultfinding*
  - Have people been personally criticized about their:
    - Leadership competence?
    - Commitment to the church?
    - Christian faithfulness?
  - Make a list of actions that could encourage confession and forgiveness for unfair criticisms.
- *Polarization*
  - What has been the result of the above actions? Is the congregation more polarized, or more unified? In hindsight, what do you wish had been done differently?
  - List ways you could avoid repeating past mistakes. Then, prioritize this list according to how important these ideas are to implement.

CHAPTER 10

Stage 5 (On Route B): Dissonant Harmony

Adversity draws men closer together and produces beauty and harmony in life's relationships, just as the cold of winter produces ice-flowers on the window-panes, which vanish with the warmth.

—Søren Kierkegaard, philosopher[1]

An Introduction to Chapter 10

As we noted at the beginning of chapter 9, the critical nature of Stage 5 requires that it be analyzed first in its negative form.

However, in this chapter we shall study Stage 5 in its positive form, where a church is headed toward harmony and change on Route B.

How Do We Get on Route B (Harmony and Change Ahead)?

ROUTE A AND ROUTE B: SOME IMPORTANT DIFFERENCES

Route A: As you remember, Route A is a sequence of stages and triggers that a church encounters when it is headed toward group exit.

Route B: This is the route a church will travel if it alters two key trigger events (Triggers 2 and 4). On this course, group exit is thwarted and, therefore, it is the preferred route for a church to undertake. However, we have not discussed how a church gets started down Route B since the first few pages of chapter 7. So

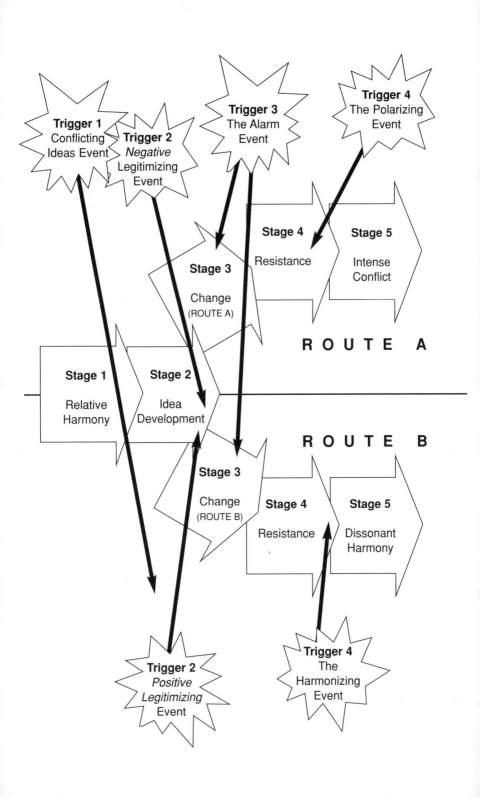

let us briefly recap how a church can get back on track and headed down the preferred Route B.

The "Positive" Legitimizing Event

A church starts down Route B when it experiences Trigger 2 as a Positive Legitimizing Event rather than a negative one. In chapter 7, we defined a Positive Legitimizing Event as an event that occurs when new ideas are "championed or legitimized by an authority figure who does so in an unhurried, prayer-infused, and deliberate manner that not only results in change, but also builds harmony between the change proponents and the status quo." If you need to reposition your church on Route B, begin by returning to chapter 7 and review how to "re-legitimize" the change process.

Three Steps to Changing the Route You Are On

For the present discussion, let's look at figure 10.1, a summary of the steps a church must undertake to readjust the route it is on.

Figure 10.1 Three Steps to Changing the Route You Are On

If you want to change from Route A (where a group will eventually exit the church) to Route B (where groups will remain with the church), you should accomplish three things before you undertake the present chapter:

1. **Go back and identify the Legitimizing Event** (Trigger 2) that began the polarization process. (See chapter 7 to identify a Trigger 2 event.)
2. **Re-legitimize the process** by creating a new and positive Legitimizing Event. Review chapter 7 to see how.
3. **Read chapters 7 and 8**. They describe how Stages 3 and 4 occur on the preferred Route B. Use the insights and exit antidotes from these chapters to reposition your church on Route B.

ARE YOU READY FOR TRIGGER 4?

If you have re-legitimized the process and are headed down Route B, then you are ready to tackle Trigger 4: the Harmonizing Event. In the last chapter, we witnessed the destructive forces that are unleashed when Trigger 4 is experienced as a Polarizing Event. In this chapter, we will look at what could take place when Trigger 4 occurs as a Harmonizing Event.

A Biblical Blueprint for Route B

Route B, where change takes place in a bipartisan manner, would certainly appear to be the preferred route. And, the scriptures give added insights into the potency and propriety of this route.

Perhaps few scripture passages jump out with such profundity as David's soliloquy to harmonious relationships in Psalm 133. Here are few brief lessons that can be garnered from this passage.

- **Tension and conflict are a byproduct of living in a fallen state**. David, the author of the psalm, was no stranger to estrangement. The constant tension between his wives, offspring, and administrative leaders indicate that David was at the epicenter of unpredictable forces. In Psalm 133:1, David seems to yearn for unity and harmony, musing "how good and pleasant it is when brothers live together in unity!" This impassioned plea of a king, who was surrounded with emotional and political fault lines, reminds us that a spiritual leader is not immune to conflict.[2] In fact, the natural position of the church within a fallen world means that Christian leaders will constantly be battling the negative forces released by tensions, disputes, and differences of opinion. Conflict is simply a result of our work environment.

- **Unity releases joy**. David goes on to extol the joys that accompany unity. Few images could be so provocative to an ancient Hebrew as the picture of "precious (anointing) oil . . .

running down on Aaron's beard, down upon the collar of his robes." David seems so smitten with the imagery that he devotes an entire verse to picturing this cascade of oil, symbolic of God's Holy Spirit. The lesson he evokes is that the bliss of unity is analogous to the elation that accompanies a deluge of God's anointing. And he is affirming that a joyful bathing in God's Spirit is what occurs when unity is present among believers. David continues the imagery with the analogy of refreshing dew falling on Mount Zion (a rare occasion in the hot summers of Israel).

- **Unity bestows God's blessing.** Probably the most astounding insight is that David, under divine inspiration, concludes the soliloquy with a declaration that God has promised to "bestow" God's blessing upon those who carefully cultivated this harmony (verse 3*c*). David even ties eternal destiny to such harmonious behavior (verse 3*d*). It seems that Psalm 133 powerfully and unequivocally promises divine assistance when Route B is adopted and embraced.

Space does not permit me to discuss other passages where unity and harmony are extolled. But it is worth mentioning that, in Ephesians 4:3, Paul uses his apostolic influence over churches in Asia Minor to stress that Christians must "*make every effort* to keep the unity of the Spirit through the bond of peace" (italics mine). The phrase "make every effort" seems to hint at the arduous and protracted effort that such unity building requires.

Exit Antidote 13: *Unity takes work.* To foster unity takes "every effort," capability, and aptitude to accomplish (Ephesians 4:3). Unity does not appear to be a natural or normal occurrence from either Old Testament examples (David's struggles) or New Testament admonitions (as in Paul's exhortation to the Ephesians). In fact, because we live in a fallen world, conflict arises more naturally than unity does. Thus, while Route A is more likely to be encountered, the preferred Route B is attainable with some hard work. Leaders willing to correct our human predilection for discord will understand that the process will take dedication, energy, information, and anointing.

A Caveat: Once on Route B, There Is No Guarantee You Will Remain There

It is important to note that simply because a church is on Route B does not guarantee that it will remain on this preferred course. Overconfidence can sometimes allow a church to slip back onto Route A, headed toward conflict and group exit.

In order to remain on Route B, it is imperative to initiate Trigger 4 as a Harmonizing Event rather than as an Alarm Event.

On Route B: Trigger 4: The Harmonizing Event

The Story of Broad Street Church

Broad Street Church had once been a thriving congregation on the edge of a metropolitan city. It was a part of a community named Oakdale, an inner suburb that, in the 1960s, had been a popular destination for the upwardly mobile.

The 1970s and 80s had not been so kind to Oakdale or Broad Street Church. The suburbanites began to flee the area because of Oakdale's proximity to the inner city. Though many residents tried to keep up the small businesses, tree-lined streets, and numerous cul-de-sacs, drugs and crime took their toll.

The church's deterioration paralleled that of the community, only at a slower pace. The church lost most of its members to the outer suburbs by the early 90s. By the mid-90s, the church was almost devoid of younger and middle-aged families. The remaining congregants were mostly retirees that either refused to or could not leave the area.

THE COMMUNITY UNDERGOES A RENAISSANCE

But things started to change for Oakdale and Broad Street Church. Young and trendy families seeking affordable housing began to move into the area in the late 1990s. The community government had driven the drug trade out of the area and now its safe streets and accessibility to downtown made Oakdale an attractive community. Soon, Generation X and Boomer families began revitalizing the area. Fashionable clothiers, cafes, and bookstores soon opened. Oakdale was undergoing a renaissance, and Broad Street Church was not far behind.

The congregation hired a gifted Boomer-age pastor named Lynn. He started moving the church toward change in a nonthreatening and cautious manner. He worked hard at building and maintaining dialogue between the change proponents and the status quo. Now that the church had started to grow with young families, the church hired me to help them map out a strategy to move from a small church of 110 (their present attendance) to a church of more than two hundred attendees.

How Broad Street Church Encountered Stages One to Four

Broad Street Church was headed down Route B, toward harmony and change. To understand Stage 5, let us recap the stages and triggers that the church went through on its journey toward harmonious change.

Stage 1: Relative Harmony. Broad Street Church experienced relative harmony, but with a dwindling congregation until Lynn was hired as the pastor. Witnessing the renaissance of the community, and urged by the church's leadership to reach younger people, Lynn began to acquaint the status quo with new ideas for change.

Trigger 1: Conflicting Ideas Event. Lynn encouraged the leaders to attend a series of three denominationally sponsored seminars over the course of a year. The seminars dealt with modern worship, innovative outreach ideas, and streamlining the leadership structure. The change proponents believed that these new ideas could save Broad Street Church, but these ideas conflicted with many of the beliefs and familiar practices of the status quo.

Stage 2: Idea Development. New ideas began to percolate within the congregational life of Broad Street Church, yet a subtle polarization was starting to take place. "I thought at the time that they would see how good these ideas were for them" one change proponent recalled. "They didn't tell us we couldn't do it." In fact, the status quo gave little indication of their displeasure, but also gave no significant indication of their support. They were either hoping Broad Street Church's change proponents would come to their senses or abandon their ideas.

Trigger 2: Legitimizing Event. Lynn lent credence to the change proponents' ideas in an unhurried and conciliatory manner. "I started two focus groups made up of newcomers who wanted to study contemporary worship and new organizational structures for the church," Lynn remembered. "Then, after they had gathered their research, I had some of our long-standing members join them to put together a plan they could take to the administrative council." As the reader will remember from chapter 7, it is imperative that a Legitimizing Event be conducted in a positive manner. Lynn orchestrated a Legitimizing Event so that it not only moved the church toward change, but also built harmony between the change proponents and the status quo.

Stage 3: Change. Change progressed at Broad Street Church in an unhurried and conciliatory way. Prayer was an integral part of the process, and permission was always attained from the proper committees and councils. A new vision statement that helped stress the overall identity of the church was drafted and adopted. As a result of these actions, neither the change proponents nor the status quo coalesced into subgroups.

Trigger 3: Alarm Event. The denomination of Broad Street Church permitted small and medium-sized churches to streamline their leadership system around a smaller administrative council and a reduced number of committees. The church council, whose majority was now comprised of change proponents, voted to implement the new simplified structure. The church's committees and boards would now be downsized into three general areas.

Status quo members on several committees sensed their long-held positions were in jeopardy. As a result, feelings began to rise among the status quo that changes at Broad Street Church were going too far, too fast. This demonstrates an important fact: Even on Route B, tension can still arise over change.

Stage 4: Resistance. Broad Street Church began Stage 4 in a way similar to Route A—special meetings were being called and votes were being taken on the issues. However, when a church is on Route A, emotions are further inflamed by these actions. Conversely, when a church is on Route B, judicious and conciliatory leadership will dampen emotions and help participants uncover common ground. Lynn expected tensions to arise over change so he stressed mutual understanding, a sharing of concerns, and conflict resolution to unify the two groups.

Exit Antidote 14: *Don't try to avoid confrontations. They are inevitable.* Special meetings and votes on issues of change are unavoidable. It will be fruitless to try and evade them. They occur on both Route A (toward conflict) and Route B (toward change). The major difference is the way in which the meetings and votes are conducted. On the route toward change they have the following characteristics: they uncover common ground, demonstrate conciliatory behavior, resolve conflict, and focus on the overall organization.

HOW BROAD STREET CHURCH ENCOUNTERED A HARMONIZING EVENT

Lynn began a series of five monthly sermons that would recount the history of the church. In preparation, Lynn pored over the church's history.

As Lynn concluded his journey, he became convinced that there were many historical parallels to the current quandary. In his sermons, he demonstrated how the church had successfully, and at times not so successfully, addressed change in the past. Slowly, the change proponents began to look at the status quo in a whole new light, discovering that many of the status quo had, at one time, been change proponents themselves! It dawned on the change proponents that the status quo were not against change but, rather, that they were not yet open to the specific change the change proponents proposed.

The status quo also benefited from Lynn's historical review. They affectionately recalled how the church had weathered many storms by choosing the common good over self-interests. This gave new hope to both the change proponents and the status quo that a bipartisan solution could be attained.

At the end of the sermon series, Lynn urged the church leaders to withdraw for a weekend retreat in order to come up with unifying ideas for change. Lynn made sure that both change proponents and the status quo were well represented at the retreat, and as a result plans were developed to implement change in unifying, and bipartisan ways.

Upon returning to the church, Lynn had the leaders organize a "Unity Sunday," where the historical strengths and the future changes of the church would be celebrated. The focus was now on the overall congregational identity, not the trifling preferences of factions. Consequently, everyone at Broad Street Church had a heightened appreciation for choosing the common good over self-interest.

The Harmonizing Event (Trigger 4)
on Route B: Harmony and Change Ahead

Now that we've observed one such Harmonizing Event, let's define, in a general manner, what is meant by Trigger 4.

On Route B: Harmony and Change Ahead

Trigger 4: The Harmonizing Event is an event or series of events that focuses on the overall congregational identity by:
- celebrating the organization;
- helping factions find common ground and develop bipartisan plans;
- stressing the common good over self-interests.

The result of this event is that factions agree to stick together despite their differences.

CHARACTERISTICS OF A HARMONIZING EVENT (TRIGGER 4)
ON ROUTE B: CHANGE AHEAD

Harmonizing Events come in many forms. However, there are some general characteristics. The events tend to:
- **Celebrate the overall organizational identity.** Harmonizing events focus on change and progress in the history of the church through:
  - a special focus in Sunday services (such as a weekly five minute "history capsule" that describes a successful event in the history of the church);
  curriculum in a newcomers' or new members' class that addresses the history of the church and how it has handled change;
  hosting speakers with a historical perspective who can speak about how change was implemented in the past in a unifying manner.

- **Establish common ground.** Harmonizing Events that create common ground can include:
  - Retreats or events where subgroups of the church fellowship, pray, and interact closely with one another;
  Bipartisan focus groups that are conducted to help members of the change proponents and the status quo bring each group's needs and concerns to the surface; these groups will also uncover areas of agreement;[3]
  Vision, mission, and personality statements can be revised or created to help the congregation focus on shared hopes, beliefs, and aspirations.

- **Laud the common good over self-interest** to help defuse factions. Methods to accomplish this include:
  - Sermons, Bible studies, and small group curriculum can investigate the selfless nature of the Christian life.[4]
    Examples of selflessness in the church's history are recounted and praised.

- **Agree for factions to stick together despite their differences.** Committing to overlook differences and stick together can be achieved by the following actions:
  - Commitment through a vow or covenant, such as membership, may be emphasized.
    Position statements on staying together as a unified congregation may be created. These position statements can alleviate much of the negative gossip and rumor that often surround times of intergroup tension.

Now, let's look at Exit Antidotes 15 and 16.

Exit Antidote 15: *Discover how your church handled change in the past.* By recalling and publicizing the positive features of these experiences, leaders can demonstrate that harmonious change is attainable. Change proponents may even discover that members of the status quo were once change proponents themselves. Thus, focusing on successful change encounters from the past can help a church fashion effective change strategies for the future.

Exit Antidote 16: *"Out of one . . . many."* Most churches grow as they find ways to focus on unity while maintaining diversity. Attempting to eradicate diversity is not only time consuming but, in all likelihood, impossible. In addition, by giving attention to the overall organization and downplaying the sectarian nature of factions, you will weaken developing fault lines. Of the many ways this can be accomplished, some of the most effective are to create or revise your vision, mission, and personality statements. This helps keep a church focused on the shared hopes, beliefs, and aspirations of its congregants.

After the occurrence of a Harmonizing Event, the church will move forward into the crucial, but often misunderstood, Stage 5: "Dissonant Harmony."

Stage 5: Dissonant Harmony on Route B (Harmony and Change Ahead)

The Story of Anderson Chapel

"The tension is not gone, but we're learning to live with it." With those words, a leader of Anderson Chapel summed up how his church encountered Stage 5 Dissonant Harmony.

Anderson Chapel was a small country church, founded in 1885 as an outreach to three small farming communities. The site, overlooking miles of fertile farmland, was chosen because of its proximity to the three towns.

Anderson Chapel was still opportunistically located. Though the three farming communities had dwindled in size, two growing midsized cities were only a thirty-minute drive to the north and the southwest. Soon, inhabitants of these two cities began descending upon the area surrounding Anderson Chapel in search of security and affordable housing. It was not long before this little country church was experiencing an influx of young families who attended Anderson Chapel because of its denominational affiliation. About the same time, a new pastor was hired.

Julia had been an associate pastor for thirteen years at a thriving church in one of the nearby cities. She had been mentored by a skilled senior minister who brought about change in diplomatic and cohesive ways. Therefore, when she arrived at Anderson Chapel she began slowly, but steadily, building what she called an "alliance for change."

The triggers and stages at Anderson Chapel were not too dissimilar from others we have studied. However, a short overview might help the reader recognize the stages of the change process.

How Anderson Chapel Encountered Stages One to Four

Stage 1: Relative Harmony. Before young people began moving to the area, Anderson Chapel enjoyed relative harmony. Those I interviewed mentioned that people "got along well" during this period. Some young families of established members did transfer their memberships to larger churches in nearby cities because of the programming they offered. But there was a general impression that this "was a good thing." A few members worried about the future, especially those related to the young families that left, but most just concentrated on the day-to-day running of the church. Because this period was not completely devoid of people exiting the congregation and resultant worries, the period could best be described as "relative harmony."

Trigger 1: Conflicting Ideas Event. A Conflicting Ideas Event occurred when a small trickle of new families joined the congregation and brought with them a new emphasis on prayer and healing. The church they left had hosted a thriving healing and prayer service. Even though that congregation in the nearby city was affiliated with the same denomination, many at Anderson Chapel were uncomfortable with this new emphasis on healing.

Soon, the new arrivals were encouraging healing activity at Anderson Chapel. A healing and prayer seminar by a nationally known speaker, formerly associated with the denomination, was held in the region. The change proponents of Anderson Chapel urged the status quo to join them in attending this seminar. None did, but many of the change proponents attended the seminar.

Stage 2: Idea Development. The change proponents returned from the seminar with a renewed desire to see a healing service at Anderson Chapel. The status quo, not wanting to dissuade these new members, tried to appease them. However, in addition, the status quo began to apply the brakes to the process, hoping the change proponents would change their minds. The change proponents did seem to lose some of their enthusiasm, until Trigger 2 occurred.

Trigger 2: *The Positive Legitimizing Event.* Then, Julia was hired as pastor. She saw the impending fragmentation of the congregation and sought to employ all of her diplomatic skills to forge what she called an alliance between the change proponents and the status quo. She deliberately met with the change proponents and explained the necessity of working through the appropriate channels. She also went to the status quo, and explained the historical perspective of their denomination, which had been known for healing services in the early twentieth century.

Julia then brought both groups together for a prayer and planning session to map out the future of the church. For weeks she urged, coached, and entreated both the status quo and the change proponents to attend the planning session. When this positive Legitimizing Event finally occurred, a wide representation of both parties united together into task groups and began to hammer out bipartisan solutions to the healing issues.

Stage 3: Change. The change proponents soon inaugurated a healing service, but they also gave in to many of the status quo's demands, and thus, their plans had a bipartisan composition. Under Julia's tutelage, both sides demonstrated conciliatory and compromising behavior.

Trigger 3: Alarm Event. Quite unexpectedly, the change proponents received an offer to host a well-known speaker on healing. Without seeking permission from the church council (and, indirectly, the status quo) the change proponents jumped at the chance to have this speaker address their prayer and healing service. Because this speaker was affiliated with a nationally known ministry, word spread quickly about his appearance.

On the Friday of the prayer and healing service, more than 175 people packed the small Anderson Chapel auditorium. This meeting was an Alarm Event to the status quo. They felt they were losing control. What would they do if all of these people started attending the church? Fear arose among the status quo that they could quickly be outnumbered and relegated to a church they did not want. The church council, which remained under the control of the status quo, called a special meeting and put the healing service on hold until certain issues could be addressed.

Stage 4: Resistance. A special meeting was called to address the council's action and, like we have seen in other examples, it was one of the best-attended meetings in years. The conciliatory mood that had permeated earlier meetings pervaded this meeting as well. Votes were taken and a modified plan was adopted so the healing service could continue with a new oversight committee. Of the six members on the new committee, two would be representatives from the council (i.e., the status quo) and the rest would be change proponents. This decision gave the change proponents a majority, but also ensured a voice for the status quo.

Trigger 4: Harmonizing Event. Julia arranged to have a leader from the denomination speak to the church on the denomination's historical relationship with healing. The gentleman spoke at the Friday healing service and on Sunday morning. He emphasized that their denomination had always placed an emphasis on healing and that miraculous healings and supernatural signs had distinguished the denomination early in its history. Both the change proponents and the status quo gained a new understanding of how the denomination had circumspectly embraced healing.

How Anderson Chapel Encountered Dissonant Harmony

Stage 5: Dissonant Harmony. Anderson Chapel now encountered the stage of Dissonant Harmony. Unlike Stage 5 on

Route A, where conflict was developing and group exit was inevitable, there were no secret meetings, ultimatums, or name-calling. Though there continued to be different opinions, there was an unspoken agreement to work out differences and stick together.

But there was tension. All change involves a degree of tension and friction. Change, by its very nature, is uncomfortable to the sedentary spirit within us. We like the familiar, and take our rest most effortlessly in the familiar. Change, when it does appear, almost always brings with it tension and strain.

This is why this stage is called "dissonant" harmony. While tension is not absent, it is tolerated.

CLOSURE HAD NOT YET BEEN REACHED

Anderson Chapel was not exempt from tension. But while tensions tend to push apart factions on Route A, at Anderson Chapel there was a high level of concession and bipartisan solutions.

Yet closure had not been attained. "We're still not together on this," confided one status quo member of Anderson Chapel, "but it's better than losing them." This lack of permanent resolution meant that, though closure had not yet been reached, the situation was somewhat acceptable. Most churches grow as they find ways to build unity among diversity.[5] The historic American motto, *E Pluribus Unum* ("out of many . . . one") could be a good maxim for the growing church.

Exit Antidote 17: *Tension will never be totally eliminated.* As long as it is not destructive, some lingering tension is acceptable. No church is going to be wholly free of conflict. All change brings about tension and friction and, even when the change process is navigated properly, different views will still be held. The description of Stage 5 as "Dissonant Harmony" reminds us that, even after successfully navigating the change process, a church will still experience some tension over opinions. Churches that accept this tension as an outgrowth of community life will not hold the church to unrealistic expectations.

I offer this final word about Stage 5 at Anderson Chapel. After the above events, I was brought in to help facilitate the church's move to a larger building. I spent three months collecting data on the congregation, its history, and its potential.

The church had spent about eighteen months in Stage 5: Dissonant Harmony. However, I noticed that, after these eighteen months in Stage 5, the church now resembled a congregation back in Stage 1: Relative Harmony. I will discuss this phenomenon in more detail in the next chapter, but typically, after a church has spent some time in Dissonant Harmony (Stage 5) it will begin a circular process and reenter Stage 1.

Once a church has navigated Stages 1 to 5, it may enter again a cycle of change, but typically with a different issue driving the process. At Anderson Chapel, this new issue turned out to be the change in facility. In fact, soon Anderson Chapel was reentering Stage 2.

Addressing change is an ongoing circular process. Therefore, a church that successfully navigates the change process once, may, at its conclusion, find itself heading down the change route again. It is important that Christian leaders learn how to repetitively navigate the change process.

Stage 5: Dissonant Harmony on Route B
(Harmony and Change Ahead)

The example of Anderson Chapel gives us a lucid picture of Stage 5: Dissonant Harmony. While this stage is largely devoid of emotional outbursts and ultimatums, it does exhibit an improving atmosphere of compromise and conciliation. Therefore, let us define Stage 5, Dissonant Harmony.

On Route B: Harmony and Change Ahead

Stage 5: Dissonant Harmony is characterized by
Harmony with:
- increasing levels of compromise;
- decreasing levels of conflict and polarization (highly emotional behavior, ultimatums, encouraging dissidents to exit, and side-taking is decreasing).

And *dissonance*, because:
- tension, differing opinions, and conflict have not been eradicated, but they are accepted.

CHARACTERISTICS OF STAGE 5: DISSONANT HARMONY
ON ROUTE B (CHANGE AHEAD)

There are many characteristics that distinguish this stage. However, a few of the most noticeable are:

- There are increasing levels of conciliation, compromise, and appeasement. This can be seen in the following actions:
  Meetings are held publicly and resolved with bipartisan solutions.
  Conflict resolution becomes characteristic of the process.

- There is less emphasis on the identity of factions and more emphasis on the overall identity of the church.
  The overall vision, mission, and personality statements of the church are created, revised, or focused upon.
  The church or denomination's history is utilized to draw unifying parallels with the current conflict.

- There is less emotional behavior.
  Decision making is not fanned by the fires of emotion.
  Ultimatums are not given.
  Dissenters are not encouraged to leave.

- Closure has not yet been reached.
  Conflict is not completely eradicated.
  Different views are still held.

The church is working out its plans for change in a bipartisan manner, which may mean that neither side is wholly satisfied with the result.

- Dissonant Harmony exists. Even though there continues to be differences of opinion, there is a tacit agreement to:
  Work out those differences that can be negotiated;
  Accept those differences that cannot be resolved.

We are almost at the end of our journey through the change process. Now we enter Stage 6, the realm where either Group Exit or Group Retention will occur.

QUESTIONS FOR GROUP STUDY, CHAPTER 10

Are You In (or Headed Into)

STAGE 5: DISSONANT HARMONY (ON ROUTE B)?

Answer the twelve questions below to discover if you are in Stage 5 "Intense Conflict" (Route A) or in Stage 5 "Dissonant Harmony" (on Route B). Place a check next to all questions that describe your congregation.

Route A (conflict and group exit ahead) Stage 5: Intense Conflict	(check if yes)	Route B (harmony and change ahead) Stage 5: Dissonant Harmony	(check if yes)
1. Highly emotional behavior	____	1. Level-headed behavior	____
2. Secret meetings	____	2. Public meetings	____
3. Increasing mention of conflict	____	3. Decreasing mention of conflict	____
4. Meetings result in sides being taken	____	4. Meetings result in compromise	____
5. The identity of factions is stressed	____	5. Church's overall identity is stressed	____
6. People encouraged to take sides	____	6. People encouraged to negotiate	____
7. Attacks are often personal	____	7. Personal attacks are rare	____

Stage 5 (On Route B): Dissonant Harmony

8. Ultimatums frequently occur ____	8. Ultimatums are rare ____
9. Factions are encouraged to leave ____	9. Factions are encouraged to stay ____
10. Conflict is not completely resolved ____	10. Conflict is not completely resolved ____
11. Different views are being voiced ____	11. Different views are being voiced ____
12. There is no closure ____	12. There is no closure ____
TOTAL (Route A) from above ____	TOTAL (Route B) from above ____

Find the total for each column. The route with the most checkmarks will likely be the route you are on. Route B, the path toward harmony and change, is the preferred route.

Remember, if you are on Route A, headed toward division and eventual group exit, you must undertake the following:

• Identify the Legitimizing Event (Trigger 2) that began the polarization process (see chapter 7 for an explanation of how to identify a Legitimizing Event).

• Re-legitimize the process by going back and creating a new and Positive Legitimizing Event. Again, return to chapter 7 to see how to create a Positive Legitimizing Event that occurs in a more deliberate, permission-seeking, and cautious way.

CHAPTER 11

Stage 6: Group Exit or Retention?

The language of friendship is not words but meanings.
—Henry David Thoreau, author and naturalist[1]

Trigger 5: The Justifying Event on Route A (Toward Conflict and Group Exit)

The Death of Third Church

Let's return briefly to Third Church, where we encountered Bill, a creative young pastor who met his match in the powerful forces of change. Bill, prepared to publicly support change, called a meeting to force a showdown with the status quo, though he was largely unaware of the forces involved. The meeting became a Polarizing Event (Trigger 4) and only further divided the status quo and the change proponents. Citing a lack of ambassadorial skills, the status quo critized Bill at the meeting. Instead of moving the church toward change, Bill found himself on the defensive, shielding himself from what he perceived as unfair accusations.

Here is a brief review of how Third Church (chapter 9) traveled down Route B (toward conflict and eventual group exit):

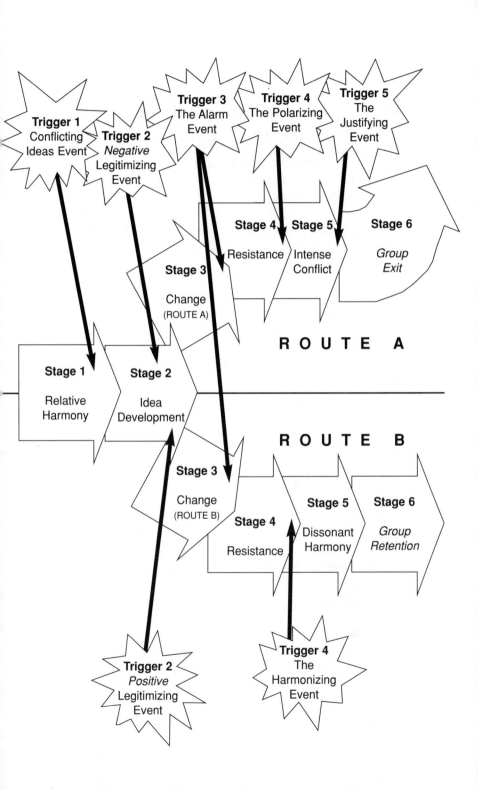

Stage 1: Relative Harmony. Prior to a youthful population surge in the area, the members of Third Church were relatively satisfied with the church's goals and achievements.

Trigger 1: Conflicting Ideas Event. Young families started attending Third Church, bringing a preference for the modern worship styles they had experienced in other churches.

Stage 2: Idea Development. The new arrivals proposed changes in worship styles that they believed would attract their youthful friends.

Trigger 2: Legitimizing Event. Bill began vocally and persistently supporting the change proponents.

Stage 3: Change. The change proponents added an 8:00 A.M. modern service and made extensive changes in the auditorium. Unable to be removed prior to the 10:45 A.M. traditional service, these changes visibly intruded into the later service. Though the status quo complained, change proponents felt they would eventually win over their detractors.

Trigger 3: Alarm Event. The change proponents pushed a motion through the administrative council that would switch the service times. To the change proponents this was not an Alarm Event, but only a natural progression in the change process. However, to the status quo, this was unquestionably an Alarm Event. It was not just the switching of the times that alarmed the status quo, it was the change proponents' newfound influence and power.

Stage 4: Resistance. Special meetings were held with a great degree of discussion but little switching of sides. Each faction became aware that they were frustrating the goals of the other, but everyone was dumbfounded as to how to resolve the escalating conflict.

Trigger 4: Polarizing Event. Bill called a special council meeting to publicly support the change proponents. However, at the meeting the status quo suggested Bill's poor diplomatic skills were the problem. Change proponents were shocked at the prospect of losing their champion. Both sides began to intensify the conflict and the controversy moved away from worship and toward Bill's leadership style. Bill resigned at the end of the meeting.

Stage 5: Intense Conflict. Both sides dug in. For the status quo, Bill's abrupt resignation confirmed his inappropriateness for the job. Change proponents felt Bill had been pushed out by the status quo and worried that they were next. As a result, both sides began to consider group exit as a possible solution.[2]

A final showdown was poised to occur with Trigger 5: the Justifying Event.

During the three months following Bill's resignation, partisan meetings took place. Most of them quickly mutated into grievance sessions. In these meetings, both factions were setting the groundwork for a final showdown.

The showdown occurred in a congregational meeting and became the Justifying Event that would push a sizeable segment of the congregation out of the church.

The change proponents had four goals they hoped to accomplish at the meeting:

1. They wanted to replace the administrative council chairperson with someone who was a change proponent.
2. They sought to replace two members of the worship committee who they felt had been overly antagonistic to their ideas.
3. They wished to elect three new members to the nominating committee so that more change proponents would be selected for influential church positions.
4. And if need be, they wanted to publicly decry the status quo's unsuitability for their positions.

Largely because of this last goal, the change proponents came prepared with a list of failures, shortcomings, and general examples of unsuitability that they had witnessed in the status quo leadership. In an attempt to persuade others, the change proponents earnestly recruited noncommitted members to attend the meeting. "Eyes will be opened," stated one change proponent in anticipation of the assembly.[3]

THE NIGHT A LINE WAS DRAWN IN THE SAND

The meeting was barely under way when the change proponents brought forth their motions. In response, the status quo told them that dismissing the administrative chairperson and members of the worship and nominating committees was highly unlikely. Anticipating this, the change proponents prepared to cite a litany of objections to the status quo's leadership.

What followed was an extremely uncomfortable meeting characterized by quotes taken out of context; perceived snubs; outright exaggerations; and some surprisingly true, but disparaging, remarks that only served to further entrench all groups.

The meeting came to a head when a status quo leader stood and called for a vote on the chairperson of the administrative council. He prefaced the vote by saying, "This vote is a line in the sand drawn by the newcomers. If you agree with them that we should throw out these dedicated Christians, then vote to remove them."

There is little wonder that the vote fell along subgroup lines, with a great number of abstentions. The noncommitted attendees who did vote were the swing vote. They voted to keep things the way they were, not wanting to offend their friends in leadership. Needless to say, the vote was in favor of retaining the chairperson.

Over the course of the next hour, votes were taken on replacing other members of the worship committee. The strategy was the same, along with the result. Sensing that an impasse was evident, change proponents left the meeting in protest after a third vote. And, in a matter of weeks, most of them left the church as well.

The Justifying Event (Trigger 5)
on Route A (Conflict and Group Exit Ahead)

Let's now define the Justifying Event.

On Route A: Conflict Ahead

Trigger 5: The Justifying Event is an event that "justifies" the departure of exit-prone groups. Four fundamental characteristics distinguish this event:
1. Change is now deemed unachievable.
2. Unity is now regarded as unattainable.
3. Common organizational identity is diminished.
4. Subgroup identity is increased.

As a result, all parties begin to consider group exit as a viable solution to the continued conflict.

CHARACTERISTICS OF A JUSTIFYING EVENT (TRIGGER 5)
ON ROUTE A (CONFLICT AHEAD)

Characteristics of Trigger 5 include, but are not limited to:
• Irrational behavior, emotions, and feelings arise that "justify," in the minds of those affected, the departure of an exit-prone group.
  Battle lines erupt with intense emotional behavior, such as: inflammatory verbiage, followed by unruly shouts of agreement or applause; accusations (personal and corporate); or criticizing a person's suitability for office.
  Actions and attacks are seen as irrevocable, with statements like: "There's too much water under the bridge," "After what's been said here, it's doubtful we can ever work together," or "That's the last straw!"
• Change is now deemed unachievable, with statements like: "There is no use fighting them," or "They'll never change."
• Unity is now regarded as unattainable, with proclamations such as: "We're too divided to stay together," or "We have differences that can't be reconciled."

- Exit is now entertained as the preferable option to continued fighting. Statements surface such as: "It will be better if we (or they) leave," or "It's the only way to bring about peace."

Stage 6: Group Exit
on Route A (Conflict Ahead)

How a Justifying Event Propels Us into Stage 6

It can be seen from the above that a Justifying Event leads to irrevocable polarization. Now, both sides begin to entertain the option that causes the least pain and estrangement—separation. The Justifying Event has accomplished its malicious work: It has justified the dissociation of the change proponents and the status quo.

Stage 6: Group Exit

CHANGE PROPONENTS EXIT THIRD CHURCH

After the meeting, there were a number of informal discussion groups in the parking lot. Within a week, a meeting had been called at the home of one of the leading change proponents. Almost all of the change proponents attended, along with a good number of noncommitted, but inquisitive, members. At this meeting, the change proponents began to strengthen their group identity. A formal breakaway organization did not yet exist, but the change proponents began to design the type of church they had always desired. "This is a blessing. It gives us the type of church we've always wanted," was the way one change proponent summed up the meetings.

As enthusiastic as the change proponents were about the future, they were also surprisingly conciliatory toward the status quo. "I've got to forgive them for the things they said and I'm sure they will forgive us. We just wanted two different things," was one summation. He was right. The status quo and the change proponents had wanted two different expressions in worship and ministry. What was regrettable was that they couldn't work together to retain bipartisan expressions in the same congregation.

THE STATUS QUO WHO REMAIN BEHIND

"It was as if we gave them the keys to the church and they didn't respect it," stated one gentleman in his sixties. "I feel betrayed." Similar expressions of disappointment, hurt, rejection, and anger were voiced by the status quo.

The atmosphere among the status quo was greatly different from the mood at the change proponents' meetings. While the change proponents looked forward to a tailor-made future, the status quo looked forward to dwindling resources, fewer members, and damaged self-esteem.

THE FALLOUT

Soon, more people than just the change proponents began resigning their positions and leaving Third Church. This reaction was, in part, a result of the depressive mood that pervaded those who remained. "I would have liked to stay here forever," said one member who had refused to take sides, but was now leaving. "But you can almost smell the stench of death. It's discouraging."

Others continued attending Third Church with an almost morose and forsaken attitude. They went through the motions, but it was evident their hearts were not present in their volunteer duties.

It was three months later that a new congregation, West County Community Church, was born. The change proponents had been busy organizing this church since the Justifying Event. But, because their reputation had been badly damaged with the denomination, they decided to begin an independent congregation.

"It's Awful! God Will Never Bless It."

Those from the status quo who remained at Third Church still felt there was a need for the change proponents to apologize. The new pastor at Third Church said, "They did a lot of damage, and they've got to own up." The status quo needed closure, some sort of admission on the change proponents' behalf that things had gotten out of hand. Unless they took responsibility for their actions, the status quo felt the new congregation was doomed to failure. "It's awful! God will never bless it," insisted one lady who remained at Third Church.

The change proponents did not share this craving for reconciliation. They were too consumed with starting a new church. They felt a euphoric sense of liberation that blinded them to the damage they had done to relationships at Third Church.

But back at Third Church, where attendance had dropped below forty, there was a sense of abandonment. "Is it possible they'll come back?" one elderly member of the status quo publicly wondered.

A new pastor was hired about a year and a half later. This new shepherd helped the dwindling congregation close Third Church. The last few services in the old building were heartrending. Longtime members of the status quo faithfully recounted the long and illustrious history of Third Church. When they came to their recent history, however, the stories were surprisingly devoid of any mention of the change proponents. The subject, even over a year later, seemed too painful to speak about.

Are You Building an Invisible Wall Around Your Church?

At Third Church, surveys were conducted to discover if their community image was damaged by the group exits. Though most people were unaware the exits occurred, a small, but significant segment recalled unfavorable hearsay. One lady summed it up best: "I've not heard very good things about Third Church."

I have labeled this phenomenon the "invisible wall." It begins when a group exit affects the church's image among community members. It may be caused in part because the status quo are likely to feel forsaken and may passionately criticize the change proponents. As a result, many community members may conclude that the change proponents are unfaithful, or that the status quo are unforgiving.

Subsequently, an invisible wall often develops around the church, thwarting visitor flow. The church may be viewed as unfriendly to young people, not open to new ideas, and/or set in its ways. Either way, the church gets a reputation for not handling change well, and this can dissuade community residents from visiting.

Once erected, an invisible wall can be a formidable barrier. It can only be overcome by a protracted period of successful change that convinces the community that the church can now assimilate newcomers and the changes they bring.

WHY DEATH IS NOT ALWAYS INEVITABLE!

Lest the reader get the wrong impression from the above examples, the death of a church after group exit is not inevitable. If a church does not slip too low in attendance, the exit process is usually survivable. Park Hills Church was one such congregation.

After losing approximately sixty change proponents in just a few months, Park Hills Church had dwindled to about eighty attendees. Still, this was an adequate number if the church's handling of change proponents could be improved in the future.

The denominational leadership began working with our firm. Together, we were able to quickly put in place a new pastor. This shepherd facilitated healing and started the change process over again, but in a more unhurried, conciliatory, and bipartisan way. In addition, Park Hills Church had two things in its favor: Park Hills Church still retained a critical mass of attendees (about eighty, though the number may vary for most churches). Thus, while a group exit did reduce the size of the congregation, it did not decimate it. Also, the church had a forward-thinking denomination who sent them a shepherd skilled in diplomacy. This pastor assisted the church in revisiting change in a more circumspect manner. Learning from their mistakes, Park Hills Church survived and eventually thrived.

The change proponents who did leave Park Hills Church found a home in a nearby congregation. In fact, they helped this congregation break through the two hundred attendance barrier.

The end result? The change process was profitable for both congregations. Was it painless? No! Was group exit the best outcome? Probably not. But even when separation occurs, it can wind up expanding the Body of Christ (recall how Paul's disagreement with Barnabas over John Mark led to dual missionary journeys in Acts 15:36-41).

Defining Stage 6: Group Exit on **Route A (Conflict and Exit Ahead)**

Now, let's define Stage 6 on Route A, where conflict and group exit is ahead.

On Route A: Conflict Ahead

Stage 6: Group Exit occurs when a subgroup exits the congregation. *Those that exit:*
- continue developing their own organizational identity;
- euphorically pursue joining or starting another congregation;
- are surprisingly conciliatory toward the status quo, but feel no pressing need to seek reconciliation.

Those that remain behind:
- feel emotionally abused, angry, abandoned, and betrayed;
- seek closure, reconciliation, and apologies;
- suffer from damaged congregational esteem due to downsizing.

CHARACTERISTICS OF A STAGE 6: GROUP EXIT
ON ROUTE A (CONFLICT AHEAD)

In Stage 6, when a subgroup leaves the church, the following characteristics are often evident. Characteristics of **the exit group:**

158

- They start developing an organizational identity by adopting a name, electing or appointing leaders, or commencing regular meetings.
- They euphorically busy themselves with starting a new church, or joining a like-minded congregation.
- They are conciliatory toward the status quo. They talk fondly about, and enjoy casual conversations with their status quo friends. They see group exit as a good solution for both factions.

Characteristics of **the group that remains**:
- They feel emotionally abused by those who left. They verbally and sometimes physically vent their anger by storming out of meetings or refusing to attend church. They do not wish to go through the change process again.
- They seek closure, reconciliation, and apologies. They have a hard time forgiving and, especially, forgetting. They are reminded daily of the new pressures that, from their viewpoint, the change proponents brought on by abandoning them.
- They suffer from damaged congregational esteem due to downsizing. They must now focus on the mundane, daily running of the church and have little time to plot the church's future. This dilemma constantly reminds them of their failure. They feel overwhelmed and overworked.

Exit Antidote 18: *Know the six stages and five triggers.* Keep in mind that an understanding of the six stages and five triggers of group exit is critical to bringing about change without polarizing either the status quo or the change proponents. Conscientious leaders will want to thoroughly investigate the stages and triggers described in this book. The study questions included at the end of each chapter will be especially helpful. These questions, along with the illustrations, graphs, and lessons included in this book, will help leaders grasp a visual, theoretical, and procedural idea of how the change and exit process can unfold in a divisive (Route A) or a unifying (Route B) manner.

Stage 6: Group Retention
on Route B (Toward Harmony and Change)

A Success Story at Broad Street Church

"WE'VE BECOME A CHURCH FOR THE AGES . . . I MEAN *ALL* AGES!"

Now let's return to the illustration of Broad Street Church we encountered in our last chapter. The occasion was a celebration in honor of Lynn's fifth anniversary as the church's senior pastor, and the church was jubilant. The congregation now numbered more than 175, compared to only about 110 attendees prior to Lynn's arrival. The future looked bright for Broad Street Church. As I stood near the front of the auditorium one Sunday morning, a lady approached me. I recognized her as a woman who had been critical of Lynn's ministry early in his career. I wondered what type of salutation she might now bear. "I didn't think we'd make it to today," she began. "But Pastor was kind to us old people, and now we've become church for the ages . . . and I mean *all* ages!"

Her transformation was welcome, yet not totally unexpected. Lynn's cautious and bipartisan strategies had brought the church down Route B, toward harmony and change. Some tension had remained but, as the reader will remember, this is to be expected. The tension did not seem to bother Lynn nor dissuade him. Lynn just kept moving Broad Street Church toward change, not allowing the pressures to thwart his enthusiasm.

A RECAP OF OUR STAGES AT BROAD STREET CHURCH

In our last chapter, we looked at Broad Street Church's journey through stages 1 to 5 toward harmony and change. However, to help the reader appreciate Stage 6, let's briefly recall how the church traveled down Route B.

Stage 1: Relative Harmony. Initially Broad Street Church experienced relative harmony, but with a dwindling congregation. Soon, growth in the community necessitated the hiring of Lynn as pastor.

Trigger 1: Conflicting Ideas Event. Lynn encouraged the leaders to attend seminars on modern worship, new outreach ideas, and streamlining the leadership structure. These new ideas resonated with the change proponents, but conflicted with the familiar practices of the status quo.

Stage 2: Idea Development. New ideas began to percolate, which change proponents felt the status quo gave them permission to pursue. Actually, the status quo were undecided and hoping the change proponents would abandon their ideas.

Trigger 2: The Legitimizing Event. Lynn organized bipartisan focus groups that would create change proposals and take them to the church council for approval. Lynn thus allowed the bipartisan focus groups and the council to be the ones to legitimize the process.

Stage 3: Change. Change progressed at Broad Street Church in an unhurried, prayer-infused, and conciliatory way. A new vision statement for the church was adopted that stressed the church's overall identity. Subsequently, neither the change proponents nor the status quo coalesced into subgroups.

Trigger 3: Alarm Event. The church council, now dominated by change proponents, voted to implement a new simplified structure for the church's boards. Status quo members, whose long-held positions were in jeopardy, began to feel that changes at Broad Street Church were going too far, too fast.

Stage 4: Resistance. Special meetings were called and votes were taken. Lynn had, however, expected tensions to arise and primed the process by stressing mutual understanding and conflict resolution. This dampened emotions, and both parties left these meetings feeling better about each other.

Trigger 4: The Harmonizing Event. Lynn culled stories from the church's history of how the church had successfully addressed change. Congregants discovered the church had weathered many storms by choosing the common good over self-interests. Subsequently, the leaders attended a bipartisan planning retreat. Upon their return, a "Unity Sunday" was held, where the historical strengths and the future changes of the church were celebrated. The focus was one on an overall congregational identity, not the minor preferences of factions.

Stage 5: Dissonant Harmony. At Broad Street Church different views continued to be held and thus a certain degree of friction persisted. But there was less conflict and taking of sides, along with a great deal more compromise and prayer. The church now entered an extended period devoid of faction building, but not without tension.

GROUP RETENTION AT BROAD STREET CHURCH
"WE COULDN'T HAVE SURVIVED WITHOUT THEM."

The change proponents remained at Broad Street Church, and it was a good thing they did. Soon, the church suffered a devastating financial blow that would have been the death knell for the church if not for its younger members. The church's Sunday school wing was condemned due to water table and sewer problems. The church leaders had been aware of the problem, but were taken aback by the severity and haste of the city's action.

The leaders discovered that the church would need a costly $225,000 renovation of the educational wing, which, except for the sanctuary, constituted almost the entire church facility. They considered what they could do without the educational wing. They could still hold church services, but Sunday school classes, children's ministries, and the church offices would have to be moved.

The church was now hovering a little above 175 in attendance and was poised to break the two hundred attendance barrier in the next year and a half. But this new financial pressure threatened to halt growth and polarize the church if not handled properly.

Again, following the practices he had employed in Trigger 4 (the Harmonizing Event), Lynn cajoled and recruited a bipartisan committee to develop a solution. The change proponents and the status quo had been accustomed to working together because Lynn had encouraged this route throughout the change process. As a result, a bipartisan group quickly convened and tendered suitable plans for raising the $225,000, as well as locating temporary space for the Sunday school two-thirds of a mile away.

Initially, many of the status quo had worried about meeting such a large capital expense. Most of the status quo were aging members of the congregation, living on fixed incomes. The change proponents, on the other hand, were entering their power years of financial growth and expansion. It was these younger change proponents who made up the lion's share of the funds needed for the renovation.

"The renovation would have killed the church if the change proponents had left," stated Lynn. "We couldn't have survived without them, and it's brought us closer too."

Lynn's summation had been an appropriate finale to this encounter with the change process.

Stage 6: Group Retention
on Route B (Harmony and Change Ahead)

Group retention is probably the easiest stage to define. It occurs when a church retains its subgroups and both groups focus on an overall organizational identity rather than individual predilections. This, in turn, unites the strengths inherent in each subgroup to build a stronger whole.

It is important to understand that change proponents and the status quo function like "subcongregations" within the overall congregation.[4] In fact, if one of these subgroups exits, it will usually move from subcongregation status, to the status of an actual congregation. However, for the current discussion, it is important for the reader to simply understand that the church can survive, and thrive, if it keeps its subgroups (or subcongregations) peacefully existing under one roof, one name, and one leadership team. George Hunter, whose probing mind readily dissects church structure, described a church as "a congregation of congregations."[5] An even more accurate definition might be "a congregation of subcongregations."[6]

With this understanding, it then becomes clear that, when subgroup retention occurs, a new entity comes into existence—"a congregation of subcongregations." This metamorphosis is not to be feared or avoided. It makes the church more flexible, adaptable, attractive, and survivable.

However, it will take work to preserve unity in the face of diversity. In the section titled "Unity Building Exercises" of *A House Divided,* I provided examples of how to foster unity in a multi-group church.[7]

Let's now define this stage of multiple subgroups coexisting in Dissonant Harmony.

On Route B: Harmony and Change Ahead

Stage 6: Group Retention occurs when multiple subgroups decide to stay together in a state of Dissonant Harmony, and each contributes their unique strengths to the whole.

CHARACTERISTICS OF A GROUP RETENTION (STAGE 6)
ON ROUTE B (CHANGE AHEAD)

Since the definition of group retention is relatively straightforward, then it stands to reason that the characteristics of Stage 6 will also be uncomplicated. The characteristics can include, but not be limited to, the following:

• Multiple subgroups decide to stay together.
    Conciliation takes place between subgroups, such as the change proponents and the status quo.
    Public attestations of commitment are held, such as a "Unity Sunday," to stress the commitment of subgroups to remain together.

- Tension is not absent, but it is managed. Churches that survive learn to live with tension that is dissonant but dominated; one where:
    Diverse opinions are voiced, and a wide variety of programs are conducted.
    New ideas continue to stretch the conflict-management systems within the church.
- Although there is dissonance, there is also harmony.
    Emotional outbursts and attacks do not commonly appear, and there is respect and tolerance for dissimilar views.
    The overall organization has become the focus.

- Each subgroup contributes its unique strengths to the whole.
    Change proponents produce culture-current ministries that attract youth-oriented people.

- Status quo members keep traditional ministries alive, which may attract traditional-minded community residents who have lost such ministries at their churches.

- Diverse programming increases the church's attractiveness to a broader range of the community.
    A greater percentage of the community can find something that attracts them to the church and families can find ministries for all age groups and preferences.
    Nuclear and extended families can find ministries for all age groups and preferences.

Why Churches Go Back to Stage 1 After Stage 6

Before we go any further, it is important to again focus on the circular process of change and group exit behavior. As we saw in the last chapter, churches in Stages 5 and 6 Dissonant Harmony, appear to slowly return to Stage 1, where the change process is likely to start all over again. The only difference is that, this time, a different force stirs up conflict.

The Treacherous Waters of Change Must Be Navigated and Subdued

A church that desires to grow must understand the circular process of change and be ready to navigate the challenging waters of change again and again. Change is fraught with challenges, predicaments, and crises. But once the route is clearly understood, and the circular nature of the process is planned for, we need not fear change—we need only to come well prepared. This leads us to our last antidote.

Exit Antidote 19: *Churches will go through the exit process again and again. Once a church has completed the process of moving from Stage 1 (Relative Harmony) through Stage 6 (Group Exit or Retention), it will usually undergo a circular process and reenter Stage 1.* It will be some new change that will push the church back into the change process, with the potential for a subgroup to exit again. Simply because a congregation has successfully navigated the exit process once does not mean it will be successful when it goes through the process again. A continual re-familiarization with the triggers and stages of group exit will be necessary throughout the life of the church if a congregation is to remain intact as it grows.

QUESTIONS FOR GROUP STUDY, CHAPTER 11

Are You In (or Headed Into)
Stage 6: Group Exit or Group Retention

Group Exit. If you answer "yes" to two or more of the following questions, you may be about to experience a group exit.

1. Has a subgroup been making changes without seeking the approval or input of the official church administration?

2. Have talented leaders resigned their positions in protest? (Even though the word "protest" may not have been used, could it be construed that certain resignations were undertaken as acts of remonstration and/or complaint.)

3. Have subgroups been holding separate meetings or starting to develop their own congregational identity?

4. Have members of the church started to accept the inevitability of a group leaving (perhaps describing the exit as "a necessary evil" or "the only workable solution")?

Do you have the critical mass necessary to survive a group exit?
The critical mass needed to sustain a dwindling church varies based upon a church's facility, polity, and leadership. However, I have developed three general guidelines to help the reader ascertain if their church has dropped below the critical mass necessary to survive a group exit. If a church retains all of the criteria below after a group exit, then the situation is usually survivable.

The three criteria for exit survivability are:
1. If the church's attendance does not fall to below 35 percent of the auditorium's comfortable seating capacity, then a church has a chance to survive. The "35 percent rule" can also be met by moving to a smaller meeting area were congregational size is 35 percent or more of a room's comfortable seating capacity. Is your church attendance less than 35 percent of the auditorium's comfortable seating capacity? If it is, quickly adjust accordingly.

2. Discover the average size of a congregation in your denomination. Multiply this number by 25 percent (or .025) to find the minimal congregational size that people usually come to expect in this denomination. If you are at or higher than this number, survival is possible.

3. Do you have a full-time pastor who is committed to remaining with the church for two or more years? At least one resolute full-time minister is usually required to survive group exit. Part-time leadership is one of the greatest destabilizing forces during the rebuilding process. Can you afford to hire a full-time shepherd? And is your current (or future) pastor committed for two or more years?

Group Retention. If you answer "yes" to two or more of the following questions, you are probably on the verge of group retention.

1. Have the leaders of your church's subgroups made public declarations of their intention to remain together and keep the church unified?

2. Have subgroups been working together on projects, ministries, events, plans, and outreach?

3. Has the church been minimizing subgroup identity and instead focusing on the organization's overall identity? What do you talk about more: the distinctiveness of subgroups, or the strengths of the overall church?

4. Are you willing to tackle the process of change and potential group exit again in order to help the church move ahead?

CHAPTER 12

Two Actions and an Attitude That Can Keep Your Change Proponents (and Your Status Quo Too!)

Each success only buys an admission ticket to a more difficult problem.
—Henry Kissinger, Nobel Prize recipient[1]

What We Have Learned

From the preceding chapters, it is clear that group exit is not only avoidable, but that the tensions that change creates can make a church more diverse and, as a result, stronger. The following are some general insights that we can glean from analyzing the change and exit process.

- Change is inevitable.
- Tensions accompany the change process.
- These accompanying tensions usually push groups apart and create "fault lines." As a result, subgroups will eventually coalesce into polarized groups with "battle lines."
- During the change process, groups often polarize into "change proponents" and the "status quo."
- Subgroups will polarize further, unless a concerted effort is made to address certain issues.
     The overall identity of the organization must be emphasized over the identity of subgroups.

Bipartisan plans must be employed to gain inclusive goal ownership.

The process must be unhurried, conciliatory, and prayer-infused.

- If a subgroup feels they are not being respected, heard, and heeded, they will consider group exit.
- If polarization continues, personal attacks and ultimatums will push a subgroup out of the congregation.
- Finally, the process appears to be circular. This means that a church that either retains or loses a group will usually return to Stage 1 and undergo the entire process again.

Sprinkled among these lessons are two key principles that influence the process greatly.

Key 1: The Stakes Are High

If the change process fails, a church will not keep pace with societal change and growth. As a result, a church may be unable to put the good news into the vernacular of the populace. A congregation that is unsuccessful in adopting judicious change may dwindle and die due to lack of results in its outreach.

A final reminder is necessary about undermining orthodoxy when adjusting methodology. As I have stated earlier, I could never condone doctrinally compromising the theology of a congregation. And I believe churches must be loyal to their historical traditions, where these traditions do not go against solid doctrine or render it ineffective. However, when our methodology is judiciously adjusted to reach a culture, the good news will not only redeem and renovate that culture, but also reinvigorate our churches.

But even when we adapt judiciously, some of that change will cause friction, tension, and uncertainly among congregants. Thus an unhurried, prayer-infused, and bipartisan strategy becomes imperative if we are to preserve unity while imparting the good news.

Key 2: The Process Is Circular

As Henry Kissinger noted in the quotation at the beginning of this chapter, successfully navigating a problem once does not mean we have completed our journey. It only means that we are now ready for another (and perhaps more arduous) excursion to begin.

In chapter 11, we saw that group exit behavior is circular in nature. Once a church has successfully, or not so successfully, made it to Stage 6, the church will soon reenter the relative harmony of Stage 1. Before long, some new change will then thrust the church out of Stage 1 into Stage 2: Idea Development. The process toward group exit or group retention will begin once more. This time around, the church will, hopefully, learn from its mistakes and not misstep again.

How We Have Learned It: The Structure of This Book

Helps Contained in This Book

To assist congregations in keeping their change proponents and their status quo, I have employed the following instructional tools:

- **A Quickstart Guide.** Chapter 2 is comprised of a "Quickstart Guide." This guide allows a church enmeshed in a battle over change to quickly discover:
  What stage the church is presently undergoing.
  What are the most important remedial steps for the church to undertake.
  What will be the next tension or controversy the church will encounter and what must be done to tackle it.

A reader should begin with the Quickstart Guide in chapter 2 when he or she encounters the change process. This guide will help you quickly analyze your situation and uncover the prescription necessary to implement change without group exit.

- **Questions for Group Study.** These questions for group or individual study are listed at the end of most chapters. They are designed to help you apply the principles discussed in each chapter to your unique situation. In addition, they can help you probe deeper into the exit process. Use these questions to acquaint leaders with the change process, build team-based change strategies, initiate dialogue, and resolve conflict.

- **18 Exit Antidotes.** These will help readers recall some of the important attitudes, strategies, and expectations that the change process will unleash. Exit antidotes also work well as the basis for a sermon series designed to acquaint a congregation with the exit process. A complete list of exit antidotes is contained in Appendix B.

- **A uniform structure in many chapters.** This design allows the reader to quickly find an appropriate event, stage, or definition within the chapter without having to page through the book. Aside from a few departures, chapters are normally arranged in the following manner.
  - An analysis of a particular "trigger," containing:
    A story that illustrates the trigger;
    A definition of the trigger;
    Characteristics of the trigger.
  - An analysis of the "stage" that results from the trigger, comprised of:
    A story that illustrates this stage at work;
    A definition of the stage;
    Common characteristics of the stage.

- **A graph of the change process.** This graph will help readers with a visual representation of how the change process unfolds. This graph is included in Appendix A. The graph also depicts how the change process can unfold on one of two courses—Route A (toward group exit) or Route B (toward change and group rentention).

Strategic Actions You Can Undertake
to Stop Group Exit

Two Actions and One Attitude That Can Prevent Group Exit

To prevent an exit of either change proponents or the status quo, it is imperative to employ two actions and embrace one attitude. I will label these indispensable actions "Strategic Actions 1 and 2" and I will call the essential mind-set a "Strategic Attitude." We will discuss them in the order they occur: Strategic Action 1, the Strategic Attitude, and Strategic Action 2.

- *Strategic Action 1: When legitimizing ideas, do so in a unifying and nondivisive way.* Our first strategic action is to ensure that Trigger 2 is a *positive* legitimizing event. Let's recall our definition of Trigger 2 in its *positive* form:

Trigger 2: A *Positive* Legitimizing Event is an event or episode where change proponents' views about change are blessed, championed, or legitimized by an authority figure; who does so in an unhurried, prayer-infused and deliberate manner that not only results in change, but also builds harmony between the change proponents and the status quo.

Review the definitions in chapter 7 on Negative and Positive Legitimizing events for more insight.

- *A Strategic Attitude: Leaders must guide the church in an unhurried, prayer-infused, and bipartisan way.* There are two requisites to successfully cultivate this attitude.

Requisite 1. This strategic attitude must begin among the church's leadership and then trickle down to all congregants.[2] Not only must this outlook be honestly embraced by a church's leadership, but the average churchgoer must also recognize that change is addressed only in an unhurried, prayer-infused, and bipartisan manner.

Requisite 2. In addition, this attitude must be reflected in all aspects of church life—sermons, curriculum, planning, Bible studies, fellowship gatherings, and retreats. Simply conducting semiregular events, sermons, or meetings on this is not sufficient. Successful cultivation of this strategic attitude will require many churches moving from what Peter Wagner calls "event-orientation to process-orientation."[3] By this, Wagner means that a church must focus on long-term goals, structure, and vision rather than the short-term event planning that so often monopolizes its time.

Cultivating this strategic attitude keeps the change process on course down Route B (toward harmony and change), and is exemplified in leaders who are:

- filled with prayer;
- unhurried;
- diplomatic;
- perceptive;
- able to control their own emotions;
- team-builders who create bipartisan planning groups;
- able to subjugate their own wishes for the good of the overall organization;
- skilled at keeping the focus on the organizational identity rather than the personality of subgroups;
- prepared to undergo the process again and again.

- ***Strategic Action 2:*** *Create Harmonizing Events rather than Polarizing Events.*

This strategic action occurs when leaders substitute a "Harmonizing Event" for a "Polarizing Event" during Trigger 4.

Again, it may be helpful to review the definitions in chapters 9 and 10 for the Polarizing Event (p. 117) and the Harmonizing Event (p. 136).

An Epilogue: The Unfinished Task

Benjamin Franklin is often remembered for his wry and witty observations. After the ratification of the U.S. Constitution, many of its architects lauded its durability. To their prognostications, Franklin quipped, "Our Constitution is in actual operation. Everything appears to promise that it will last, but in this world nothing can be said to be certain but death and taxes."[4] Considering that the Bill of Rights was added four years later, and after what the reader has witnessed regarding change, the words " . . . and change" might be added to Franklin's retort.

Most students of church history are well versed about how the church has failed to culturally adapt while maintaining theological consistency. Wars, inquisitions, diets, and defrockings have resulted when the change process is not handled appropriately. Regrettably, the most heinous result of this may be the distorted image a watching world is given.

At times, such missteps have actually expanded the coverage of the good news. We noted how Paul's disagreement with Barnabas over taking John Mark resulted in two missionary journeys instead of one. In all probability, there was twice the result.[5]

Still, our Master has called upon the church to model a unified image that might elicit, from our onlookers, a desire to affiliate with us and accept God's mandates. Toward this end, Christ's admonition in John 17:20, 21 is pivotal.

"I am not praying only for these men
but for all those who will believe in me through their message,
that they may all be one. . . .
I have given them the honour that you gave me,
that they may be one, as we are one—I in them and you in me,
that they may grow complete into one,
so that the world may realise that you sent me. . . ."
—John 17:20-21 (JBP)

These words contain our motivation for managing the change process and the group exit behavior that can accompany it. Our goal is to unite in the face of diversity, subjugating our personal and petty predelictions to the unity of the believers. As a result, the church can become a model to the world of conciliation, diplomacy, patience, and conflict resolution—all in the midst of change!

Therefore, these words of our Lord serve to sustain us through the travail and struggle of our encounters with the circular nature of change. They remind us that our effort is not in vain, for our unity testifies to the world that the Lord can empower us to resist natural tendencies toward polarization as we lead the church forward in a strategic and successful manner. This book is dedicated to all leaders who will attempt such endeavors.

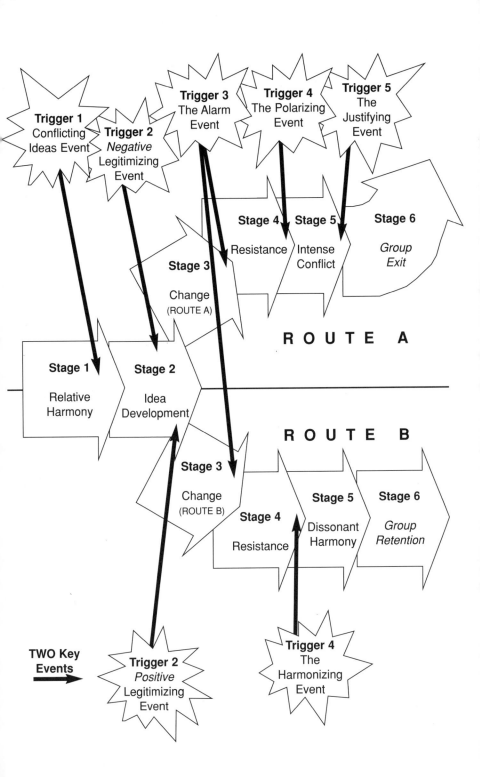

How Group Exit Occurs (and Why)

Stage 1: Relative Harmony. In this stage a congregation exhibits the three "C's." The congregation is living contented, in concord, but with some conflict.

- **Contented.** Congregants are relatively content or satisfied with the church's ministries, direction, and purpose.
- In **Concord.** The congregation focuses more on what holds them together than what pulls them apart.
- With some **Conflict.** Conflict and tensions occasionally arise, but the congregation works to keep them from causing division. Thus this stage is labeled "relative" harmony.

Trigger 1: The Conflicting Ideas Event. Attendees of a church are exposed to an idea generating event (e.g., a seminar, a book, a lecture, a former church, a friend, etc.) where they pick up new ideas that they feel should be implemented at the church they attend. These ideas conflict with ideas held by the status quo.

Stage 2: Idea Development. New ideas begin to develop within the congregation. A subtle polarization begins to take place, but groups do not yet coalesce. Change proponents patiently hope that others will come to their senses and abandon their new ideas.

ROUTE A leads to group exit. Route A results when Trigger 2 occurs as a "Negative Legitimizing Event." The result of Route A is that a group will eventually exit the church.

ROUTE B leads to group retention. Route B results when Trigger 2 occurs as a "Positive Legitimizing Event." The result of Route B is that group exits are prevented.

Trigger 2: The *Negative* Legitimizing Event is an event or episode where change proponents' views on change are inadvertently blessed, championed, or legitimized by an authority figure, and results in polarization between the change proponents and the status quo.

Trigger 2: The *Positive* Legitimizing Event is an event or episode where change proponents' views about change are blessed, championed, or legitimized by an authority figure; who does so in an unhurried, prayer-infused, and deliberate manner that not only results in change, but also builds harmony between the change proponents and the status quo.

Stage 3: Change. This is a period where change proponents begin to coalesce into an identifiable subgoup within the congregation. In addition, early, but limited, success raises the change proponents' expectations that they will be able to implement wide-ranging change.

Stage 3: Change. New ideas are introduced in a unhurried, judicious, and conciliatory way. Prayer accompanies the process, permission is sought, and the identity of the total church is stressed. Consequently, change proponents do not begin to coalesce into a subgroup.

Trigger 3: The Alarm Event is a wake-up call to the status quo that the change proponents have, in the status quo's minds, gone too far. *The status quo then galvanize into a subgroup.*

Trigger 3: The Alarm Event is a wake-up call to the status quo that the change proponents have, in the status quo's minds, gone too far. *The status quo cease to exhibit tolerance.*

Stage 4: Resistance. The status quo see the organization as facing a crisis and seek to keep the change proponents in check. Conversely, the change proponents see the organization as facing an opportunity. Spirited discussions take place, special meetings are held, and votes are taken. *Unique to Route A, Conflict Ahead: Each side argues for the legitimacy of their views, and sides are expected to be taken. These tensions only stir up emotions. Though meetings are called, there is little switching of sides. Both sides are aware they are frustrating the goals of the other, but each hopes a peaceful resolution will take place.*

Stage 4: Resistance. The status quo see the organization as facing a crisis and seek to keep the change proponents in check. Conversely, the change proponents see the organization as facing an opportunity. Spirited discussions take place, special meetings are held, and votes are taken. *Unique to Route B, Harmony and Change Ahead: There is a high degree of compromise, concession, and conciliation; resulting in multifaceted plans that meet the needs of both groups. As a result, both sides work out their conflicts.*

Trigger 4: The Polarizing Event is an event usually public, that causes both the status quo and the change proponents to feel they have received a personal attack and been unfairly treated. It transforms the *point of focus* of the conflict from specific actions to general attitudes, and results in uncompromising polarization on both sides that can lead to *permanent* solutions. This event may be characterized by personal criticisms, inflexible positions, public condemnation, pastoral resignation or removal, or binding votes limiting the influence of certain groups.

Trigger 4: The Harmonizing Event is an event or series of events that focuses on the overall congregational identity by celebrating the organization, helping factions find common ground and develop bipartisan plans, and stressing the common good over self-interests. The result of this event is that factions agree to stick together despite their differences.

Stage 5: Intense Conflict is characterized by entrenchment and fault-finding. Each side refuses to compromise or concede for fear of losing ground. Emotional outbursts (publicly, privately, and in written form) question the competence of the leadership, while ultimatums taunt the other group to leave. Fault lines have now become battle lines.

Stage 5: Dissonant Harmony is characterized by *harmony* with:
• increasing levels of compromise;
• decreasing levels of conflict and polarization (highly emotional behavior decreases).
And *dissonance*, because:
• tension and differing opinions have not been eradicated, but they are accepted.

Trigger 5: The Justifying Event is an event that "justifies" the departure of exit-prone groups. Four characteristics include:
1. Change is now regarded as unachievable.
2. Unity is deemed as unattainable.
3. Common organizational identity is diminishing.
4. Subgroup identity is increasing.
   As a result, all parties now begin to consider exit as a viable solution to continued conflict.

Trigger 5: (does not occur on Route B).

Stage 6: Group Exit occurs when a subgroup exits the church. *Those that exit:*
• continue developing their own organizational identity;
• euphorically pursue joining or starting another congregation;
• feel no pressing need to seek reconciliation.

Those that remain behind:
• feel emotionally abused, angry, abandoned, and betrayed;
• seek closure and apologies;
• suffer damaged congregational esteem due to downsizing.

Stage 6: Group Retention occurs when multiple subgroups decide to stay together in a state of dissonant harmony, and each contributes its unique strengths to the whole.

A Recap of Our *Exit Antidotes*

Exit Antidote 1: New ideas are usually germinated from a sincere desire to see a church increase or improve its ministry.
Rarely, but on occasion (see the disclaimer in chapter 7), do people suggest change simply for the sake of newness. Most often, church attendees seek to implement new ideas because they genuinely believe change will augment and expand a church's ministry. Keep in mind this goodhearted motivation, and be careful not to disparage new ideas because of the discomfort that newness always conveys. If you are uncomfortable with ideas being proposed, give them some initial latitude and spend time in prayer regarding them. Ask God to change your opinion or their point of view. Often the fruit of new ideas and/or of prayer can help change, or moderate perspectives. (See chapter 6 for details.)

Exit Antidote 2: Leaders may so desperately want to save a dwindling or aging church that they may overstate to change proponents the status quo's willingness to accept change.
Therefore if you are attempting to bring change to a congregation that is concerned about future viability, proceed at a pace that is

somewhat slower than the status quo is encouraging. Though this restraint may be hard to marshal, it will prevent the onset of polarization. (See chapter 7 for details.)

Exit Antidote 3: The church leader is expected to keep the "other" side in line. Both the change proponents and the status quo expect the pastor or church leader to keep both factions on the same team. A pastor or leader who too highly identifies with one party, in lieu of the other will only further exacerbate the faultlines that can become battlelines. Diplomacy dictates the leader be a moderator and facilitator of unity. (See chapter 7 for details.)

Exit Antidote 4: Authority figures must be careful about what they say, as well as when they say it. This is especially true during the change process. Caution, discretion, and judicious behavior are needed to offset hasty implementation of new ideas (and haste usually fosters division). (See chapter 7 for details.)

Exit Antidote 5: When advocating new ideas, encourage your listeners to be tactful and cautious. Build caution and diplomacy into seminars, sermons, lectures, and books. Enthusiastic participants may return to their congregations and inadvertently legitimize or too boldly press for the new ideas they have learned. (See chapter 7 for details.)

Exit Antidote 6: Alarm events are an unavoidable part of the change process—you cannot avoid them, but you can plan for them. An alarm event (Trigger 3) is a wake-up call to the status quo that the change proponents have gone too far with some change. This alarms the status quo and they will either galvanize into a faction themselves or at the very least cease to exhibit tolerance. Such events are usually an inescapable part of the change process. Humankind has a propensity for going too far, too fast. Expect these skirmishes to arise whenever a change process is initiated. But, if both sides prepare themselves beforehand not to overreact and to work out any problems with conciliation, forgiveness, and in a bipartisan spirit, then the divisive effects of an alarm event can be neutralized. (See chapter 8 for details.)

Exit Antidote 7: Discourage the temptation to make middle-of-the-road congregants take sides over change issues. During Stage 4, resistance, factions may attempt to bolster their perspective by recruiting middle-of-the-road people to their cause. However politicking these noncommitted individuals will polarize a larger portion of the church and eventually make bipartisan plans for change harder to achieve. In addition, because such actions stress group identity over overall organizational (church) identity, the conscripting of middle-of-the-road congregants will work against unity. And finally, such enlistment is unfair to middle-of-the-road congregants who due to personal needs, may need to circumnavigate skirmishes. (See chapter 8 for details.)

Exit Antidote 8: Learn how to re-legitimize the change process. If your church is starting to experience a polarization between change proponents and the status quo (see chapter 8 for details), do three things:
- Identify the Legitimizing Event (Trigger 2) that began the polarization process.
- Re-legitimize the process by going back and creating a *new* Legitimizing Event. At this point it will be helpful to return to chapter 7 to see how to create a *positive* legitimizing event that occurs in a more deliberate, permission-seeking, cautious and prudent way.
- Next, read (or reread if you are not on the Quickstart plan) the portions of chapters 7 and 8 that describe how Stages 3 and 4 occur on Route B, where change and harmony are ahead. Use the insights and Exit Antidotes from these chapters to reposition your church on Route B.

Exit Antidote 9: Don't think the solution is to just educate the other side. Both change proponents and the status quo must be careful not to assume that the "other side" simply needs "to be educated" for them to change their opinions. Oftentimes seminars, workshops, books, videos, etc., will be seen as tools to re-educate a faction that is hesitant. In actuality what is missing is not lack of instruction, but lack of preparation for the acceptance of new ideas. Therefore, do not count on training tools as the remedy, but rather foster dialogue, compromise, and patience, allowing a bipartisan solution on change to emerge. (See chapter 9 for details.)

Exit Antidote 10: Watch out for the sucker punch. The effective church leader will be wary of the ecclesiastical "sucker punch." This is a situation where an antagonist, either consciously or unconsciously, tries to elicit a passionate and imprudent response from a leader. A leader who "resigns in protest" is one such example. Such actions are guilt producing events that further estrange factions. Therefore, leaders must come to potentially divisive meetings with emotional energies under control. Do not let passions erupt into poor decisions. Check your emotions at the door, or don't go. (See chapter 9 for details.)

Exit Antidote 11: You are not necessarily the "next in line" to get mistreated. During the change process, simply because someone has been mistreated (fired, asked to leave, forced to resign, or otherwise ill-treated) does not mean you are next. Oftentimes, those behind such mistreatment will sense the unjust nature of their action and be less likely to repeat it in the near future. Therefore, if ill-treatment has recently taken place, an opportunity for concession and conciliation may be at hand. (See chapter 9 for details.)

Exit Antidote 12: Unity takes work. To foster unity takes "every effort," capability and aptitude to accomplish (Ephesians 4:3). Unity does not appear to be a natural nor normal occurrence from either Old Testament examples (David's struggles) or New Testament admonitions (as in Paul's exhortation to the Ephesians). In fact, because we live in a fallen world, conflict arises more naturally than unity. Thus while Route A is more likely to be encountered, the preferred Route B is attainable, but it will take work. Leaders willing to correct our human predilection for discord will

understand that the process will take dedication, energy, information, and anointing. (See chapter 10 for details.)

Exit Antidote 13: Don't try to avoid confrontations, they are inevitable. Special meetings and votes on issues of change are unavoidable. It will be fruitless to evade them. They occur on both Route A (toward conflict) *and* Route B (toward change). The major difference is the way in which the meetings and votes are conducted. On the route toward change they have the following characteristics:

- They uncover common ground.
- They demonstrate conciliatory behavior.
- They resolve conflict.
- They focus on the overall organization.

As a result the church can serve as a model of conflict resolution and unity building. (See chapter 10 for details.)

Exit Antidote 14: Discover how your church handled change in the past. It will often be helpful to uncover in a church's history times when it has successfully navigated the change process. Then by recalling and publicizing the positive features of these experiences, leaders can demonstrate that not only is harmonious change inevitable, but also attainable. Change proponents may even discover that the status quo were once change proponents themselves. Furthermore, such scrutiny will usually reveal that past experiences were characterized by unhurried, conciliatory, and prayer-infused strategies. Thus, focusing on successful change encounters from the past can help a church fashion effective change strategies for the future. (See chapter 10 for details.)

Exit Antidote 15: "Out of one . . . many." Most churches grow as they find ways to focus on unity while maintaining diversity. Attempting to eradicate diversity is not only time consuming, but in all likelihood also impossible. In addition, by giving attention to the overall organization and downplaying the sectarian nature of factions, you will weaken developing fault lines. Of the many ways this can be accomplished, some of the most effective are to create, revise and/or revisit your vision, mission, and personality statements. This helps keep a church focused on the shared hopes, beliefs, and aspirations of its congregants. (See chapter 10 for details.)

Exit Antidote 16: Tension will never be totally eliminated. As long as it is not maladaptive, some lingering tension is okay. No church is going to be wholly free of conflict. All change brings about tension and friction, and therefore even when the change process is navigated properly, different views will still be held. The description of Stage 5 as "dissonant harmony" reminds us that even after successfully navigating the change process, a church will still experience some tension over opinions. Churches that accept this tension as an outgrowth of community life will not hold the church to unrealistic expectations. (See chapter 10 for details.)

Exit Antidote 17: Know the six stages and five triggers. Keep in mind that an understanding of the six stages of group exit (and the five triggers) are critical to bringing about change without polarizing either the status quo or the change proponents. Conscientious leaders will want to investigate thoroughly the stages and triggers described in this book. Especially helpful will be the study questions included at the end of each chapter. These questions, along with the included illustrations, graphs, and lessons, will help leaders grasp a visual, theoretical, and procedural idea of how the change and exit process can unfold in divisive (Route A) or in unifying (Route B) ways. (See chapter 11, as well as chapters 5-10, for details.)

Exit Antidote 18: Churches will go through the exit process again and again. Once an organization has completed the process of moving from Stage 1 (Relative Harmony) through Stage 6 (group exit or retention), a church will usually undergo a circular process and reenter Stage 1: Relative Harmony. On this second time around it will be some new change that will push the church back into the change process, with the potential for a subgroup to exit again. Simply because a congregation has successfully navigated the exit process *once* does not mean it will be successful when it goes through the process again. A continual refamiliarization with the triggers and stages of group exit will be necessary *throughout the life of the church* if a congregation is to remain intact as it grows. (See chapter 11 for details.)

NOTES

Preface

1. Arnold Toynbee, *A Study of History* (London: Oxford University Press, 1946).

Acknowledgments

1. Early in my seminary career, Emil Brunner acquainted me with the church in two manifestations. He pointed out, in *The Misunderstanding of the Church*, trans. Harold Knight (London: Lutterworth Press, 1952), 10-19, that while, historically, the church was looked upon as an institution or organization, reformers such as Luther and Calvin saw a community built on relationships. This is what Brunner called the "hidden" or "invisible" church. This understanding of the church, as both an organization that needs to be managed as well as a spiritual community that thrives through divine guidance, has been the dual thrust that this and my previous writings have attempted to unite.

Chapter One: A New Understanding of an Old Problem

1. Donald A. McGavran, *Effective Evangelism: A Theological Mandate* (Phillipsburg, N.J.: Presbyterian and Reformed Publishing Co., 1988), 116.
2. In the 1980s and 1990s, some denominations started new churches to

provide a denominational home for groups who had exited a church due to the mismanagement of the change process. Unfortunately, this strategy had two disappointing outcomes. First, those who exited a congregation received the impression that change was best handled through distance and dissociation. Second, the traditionalists (i.e., the status quo) who remained in the church found themselves witnessing the slow death of their beloved congregation. Both of these outcomes lead me to believe that a strategy with staying power is the preferable outcome in many church situations.

3. C. Peter Wagner, *Our Kind of People: The Ethical Dimensions of Church Growth in America* (Atlanta: John Knox Press, 1979), 51. Though Wagner is not expressly referring to the local church, but the church in general, the analogy is equally valid for the local church seeking to maintain the flavorful and appetizing mixture that results from retaining both its change proponents and the status quo.

4. Donald A. McGavran, *Effective Evangelism,* 116.

5. Bruno Dyck and Frederick A. Starke, "The Formation of Breakaway Organizations: Observations and a Process Model," *Administrative Science Quarterly 44* (Ithaca, N.Y.: Johnson Graduate School of Management, Cornell University, 1999): 792-822; "Upheavals in Congregations: The Causes and Outcomes of Splits" *Review of Religious Research* 38 (New York: Religious Research Association, 1996): 159-74.

Chapter Two: A Quickstart Guide: How to Use This Book

1. Theodore Roosevelt, *The Bully Pulpit*, ed. H. Paul Jeffers, 1998.

2. To understand the unique characteristics of each of the three basic building-blocks of church structure—small groups (primary groups), subcongregations (secondary groups), and tertiary groups (congregations)—see the expanded discussion in Bob Whitesel and Kent R. Hunter's *A House Divided: Bridging the Generation Gaps in Your Church* (Nashville: Abingdon Press, 2000), 25-27.

3. Whitesel and Hunter, 31-32.

4. Ibid., 82-90.

5. Margaret Mead, *Culture and Commitment: A Study of the Generation Gap* (Garden City, N.Y.: Doubleday, 1970), 2.

6. For an in-depth look at the preferences and attitudes of different generations, see chapter 3: "Attitudes That Produce the [Generation] Gaps" in *A House Divided*, 56 ff.

7. George Barna, *The Invisible Generation: Baby Busters* (Glendale, Calif.: Barna Research Group, 1992), 157-66.

8. At times, there may be individuals or even groups that seek to bring about change, not for the cultural adaptation of Christian ministry, but solely for the sake of change. For these groups, newness, simply because it is "new," is preferred. They are motivated by originality and novelty, not by updated strategies.

For these people, even change in theological doctrine is preferred because change is always better than remaining the same. This type of change is not widely seen in churches, but it has its genesis in the concept that newness is always preferable to sameness. This perspective, though rare, must be cautiously guarded against, since undermining orthodox doctrine simply for the sake of novelty is dangerous. The orthodox beliefs and sacraments of a denomination are not part of the agenda of change proponents as I am describing them here.

9. Bruno Dyck and Frederick A. Starke, "The Formation of Breakaway Organizations: Observations and a Process Model," *Administrative Science Quarterly 44* (Ithaca, N.Y.: Johnson Graduate School of Management, Cornell University, 1999): 811-16.

Chapter Three: The Pain (and Gain) of Exits

1. Carl G. Jung, "Memories, Dreams, Reflections," Atlantic Monthly Press, 62.

2. Eddie Gibbs, *I Believe in Church Growth* (Grand Rapids, Mich.: William B. Eerdmans, 1981), 399.

3. To learn how to readily communicate your church's strengths and vision throughout your community see "STEP 1: Envision Your Leadership, Church and Community" in Bob Whitesel and Kent R. Hunter's *A House Divided: Bridging the Generation Gaps in Your Church* (Nashville: Abingdon Press, 2000), 119-20.

4. Howard C Kunreuther, "Protective Decisions: Fear or Prudence," in *Wharton on Making Decisions*, ed. Stephen J. Hoch and Howard C. Kunreuther with Robert E. Gunther (New York: John Wiley and Sons, Inc., 2001), 261.

Chapter Four: A Tale of One Church in Two Parts

1. Friedrich Nietzsche, *The Wanderer and His Shadow*, 1880.

2. Recently, "modern" has become the favored designation for what formerly was called a "contemporary" worship service. This type of service is usually characterized by upbeat music accompanied by popular instruments such as keyboards, guitars, and drums. The label "contemporary" is a bit of a misnomer, since "contemporary" means in keeping with the latest trends. Many so-called contemporary services utilize a folk-rock style that most unchurched people would not necessarily label as the latest trend. However, the terms "modern" and "postmodern" (and their cognates modernity and postmodernity) have become accepted sociological terms to describe Baby Boomer and Generation X cultural preferences. Some are even describing the preferences of the Millennials as "post-post modern" (see "Enemies in the Post-Postmodern Era—Unless . . ." by Brad Sargent in *Strategies for Today's Leader* 38, no. 1, 23-25). Therefore, for clarity, the author will utilize the more precise designation of "modern" when

referring to a folk-rock style service and "traditional" when referring to a service that is in keeping with the liturgical traditions of the church's history. In addition, worship services aimed at Generation X will be called "postmodern" celebrations and those designed to appeal to the Gen. Y will be, until a better designation arises, called "post-postmodern" worship expressions.

Chapter Five: Stage 1: Relative Harmony

1. D. H. Lawrence, *The Letters of D. H. Lawrence vol. 2,* eds. George J. Zytaruk and James T. Boulton, 1981.
2. This is an actual quote from the 1930 church history of First United Methodist Church in Attica, Indiana.
3. Lyle E. Schaller, *The Multiple Staff and the Larger Church* (Nashville: Abingdon Press, 1980), 28-31.
4. Some congregations will want to decide whether to count attendees or members. Usually, counting attendees yields a more reliable indicator of church health and growth since many churches do not purge inactive members from their rolls on a regular basis. On the other hand, counting attendees can be challenging. The questions of what ages to count, when to count, and how often to count are important to consider. Concrete suggestions for how to do this easily and consistently are put forth in a easy three-step process in Bob Whitesel and Kent R. Hunter's *A House Divided: Bridging the Generation Gaps in Your Church* (Nashville: Abingdon Press, 2000), 215-18.
5. In mathematics, when you subtract a negative number, the two negatives will make a positive. Thus, the difference between +14.9 and a −1.5 is 16.4.
6. J. Timothy Ahlen and J. V. Thomas, *One Church, Many Congregations: The Key Church Strategy* (Nashville: Abingdon Press, 1999).
7. Whitesel and Hunter, *A House Divided,* 210-11 offers sample survey questions that can help you poll a congregation and uncover its generational proportions.

Chapter Six: Stage 2: When New Ideas Are Introduced

1. Niccolo Machiavelli, *The Prince,* trans. W. K. Marriot, 1992.
2. The formidable tension generated by preferences in worship styles has been wryly described as the power behind "the first murder in human history (which) seems to have taken place between brothers (Cain and Abel) in a disagreement over worship." Elmer Towns and Warren Bird, *Into the Future: Turning Today's Church Trends into Tomorrow's Opportunities* (Grand Rapids, Mich.: Fleming H. Revell, 2000), 134.
3. To learn more about how modern, postmodern, and traditional worship services can peacefully coexist in the same church, see chapter 8, "Worship in a Tri-generational Format" in Bob Whitesel and Kent R. Hunter's *A House*

Divided: Bridging the Generation Gaps in Your Church (Nashville: Abingdon Press, 2000), 215-18.

4. Cells are characterized by intimacy and interpersonal involvement. They are not limited to "cell churches" within the cell group movement, for these intimacy-building groups are found in all congregations. They have been described by Larry Richards as "the basic building block of the life of the gathered church" and defined as "eight or twelve believers gathered to minister to each other, to grow in their sensed love and unity, and to encourage one another to full commitment to Christ." Larry O. Richards, *A New Face for the Church* (Grand Rapids, Mich.: Zondervan, 1970), 152-55.

5. A common complaint about the Willow Creek approach is that Sunday morning attendees are not afforded an opportunity to worship, because the music is delivered in a concert format. This format is employed because its leaders feel Sunday morning is one of the best times to reach nonchurched people. However, worship is not ignored. The Willow Creek model includes a midweek worship celebration, often called "New Community," that incorporates an extended time of teaching and worship and resembles the Sunday worship services of most churches. For a detailed explanation and historical overview of the Willow Creek model, see Lynne and Bill Hybels, *Rediscovering Church: The Story and Vision of Willow Creek Community Church* (Grand Rapids, Mich.: Zondervan, 1995).

6. The number of new ideas available to churches is staggering. However, in *The New Apostolic Churches: Rediscovering the New Testament Model of Leadership and Why It Is God's Desire for the Church Today* (Ventura, Calif.: Regal Books, 1998), editor C. Peter Wagner ties these ideas into helpful categories. For a valuable categorical overview by one of sharpest minds in church leadership, consult this handy volume.

7. The attitude of the status quo that change proponents will come to their senses and forsake their new ideas often surfaces over the issue of worship. Sometimes, the status quo will advocate that firsthand, repetitive experience with traditional forms of worship will change or alter the change proponents' preferences. However, because worship has, at its heart, a liturgical expression that must be indigenous to the worshiper, the hoped-for transformation usually does not occur.

Chapter Seven: Stage 3: Change

1. Benjamin Franklin, *Poor Richard's Almanac*, 1736.

2. For an engaging, but somewhat scholarly discussion of how new leaders often exacerbate or create "fault lines," see the research by Dora Lau and J. Keith Murnighan in "Demographic Diversity and Faultlines: The Compositional Dynamics of Organizational Groups" in *Academy of Management Review 23* (Linthicum, Md.: Cadmus Professional Communications, 1998): 325-40.

3. Bruno Dyck and Frederick A. Starke, "The Formation of Breakaway Organizations: Observations and a Process Model," *Administrative Science*

Quarterly 44 (Ithaca, N.Y.: Johnson Graduate School of Management, Cornell University, 1999): 812-13.

4. There has been a great deal of confusion over what constitutes a church's philosophy of ministry statement, mission statement, and vision statement. In *A House Divided*, pp. 107, 108, I have graphed the differences between these terms as described by George Barna, Elmer Towns, and myself. For the present reader, the following is a brief overview of these three types of statements:

• A *personality statement* is an extended description of the personality of a church, often seven to twenty paragraphs long. It answers the question, "Who are we, uniquely?"

• A *mission statement* is a simple, yet broad, statement that answers the question, "What do we do?" George Barna calls this the philosophic statement that undergirds the heart of your ministry. Elmer Towns further defines this as your church's ministry emphasis and church gifting. "To know Him and make Him known," "To reach the lost at any cost," and "To evangelize, exalt, edify, and equip" are examples of mission statements, according to Barna.

• A *vision statement* answers the question, "Where do we believe God is calling our church to go in the future?" George Barna and Elmer Towns refer to this as a clear mental image of a preferable future imparted by God and based on an accurate understanding of God, self, and circumstances. The characteristic that separates a *vision* statement from a *mission* statement is that a vision statement is unique to the individual church. It describes one church and usually cannot be applied to a different congregation. The author has combined the insights of Barna and Towns into eight steps that a church can utilize when writing a vision statement. These eight steps, along with examples of vision statements, can be found in Whitesel and Hunter's *A House Divided*, 108, 109.

Chapter Eight: Stage 4: Resistance

1. Eleanor Roosevelt, in a letter to Carrie Chapman Catt dated April 18, 1936, from *Eleanor and Franklin,* by Joseph P. Lash (New York: Norton, 1971).

2. Eddie Gibbs, *Church Next: Quantum Changes in How We Do Ministry* (Downers Grove, Ill.: InterVarsity Press, 2000), 237.

Chapter Nine: Stage 5 (On Route A): Intense Conflict

1. Martin Luther King Jr., sermon at Dexter Avenue Baptist Church, Montgomery, Ala., April 12, 1957.

2. Lyle E. Schaller, *Effective Church Planning* (Nashville: Abingdon Press, 1981), 150-51.

3. It is God's Holy Spirit, actively working in the believer, that brings about this conviction of ill treatment (John 16:8). Prayer becomes, as always, a key

ingredient in the change process. Prayer must be rendered in order to release God's power to convict us of our wrong actions. Therefore, if God's Holy Spirit is active in the process, it will moderate the process and curb excessive behavior (1 John 1:9).

Chapter Ten: Stage 5 (On Route B): Dissonant Harmony

1. Søren Kierkegaard, *The Journals of Soren Kierkegaard*, ed. and trans. Alexander Dru, 1938.

2. C. Peter Wagner, in his foundational book on church growth and leadership *Your Church Can Grow* (Ventura, Calif.: Regal Books, 1976), 66-67, describes the "rough road to leadership" which many famous pastors have trod. Citing examples in the lives of W. A. Criswell (First Baptist Church, Dallas, Tex.) and Robert Schuller (Crystal Cathedral, Garden Grove, Calif.), Wagner reminds us that even successful leaders must conquer outbreaks of conflict. In addition, Jerry Falwell and Elmer Towns tender an insightful look into how God used conflict to develop Falwell's leadership skills early in his career. Their *Stepping Out on Faith* (Wheaton, Ill.: Tyndale House Publishers, 1984) is an inspiring journey through Falwell's youthful career along with the careers of ten other pastors.

3. Conducting a successful focus group requires an understanding of the group dynamics involved so that the exercise will not be manipulative. For an overview of focus group basics and how to conduct a successful focus group, see Whitesel and Hunter, *A House Divided,* 151-55 and figures 7.3, 7.4, and 7.5.

4. Books such as Dietrich Bonhoeffer's *Life Together*, trans. John W. Doberstein (New York: Harper and Row, 1954); and Peter Marshall & David Manuel's *The Light and the Glory* (Old Tappan, N.J.: Fleming H. Revel Company, 1977), are good sources for illustrative stories that recount selfless actions in Christian communities.

5. Chapters 1–4 in Whitesel and Hunter's *A House Divided* explain how most churches with less than two hundred attendees will only grow if they start to cultivate several subcongregations within the overall general congregation. These subcongregations are usually organized around different generations (Builders, Boomers, Generation X, and the Millennials). They are almost like subcultures within the church. This does not mean they stray from the church's theological orthodoxy, but such subcongregations seek their own ministries, their own leaders, and their own cultural expressions. Since cultivating such subcongregations is necessary for the survival of many churches, it becomes necessary to ensure we find ways to build unity among this diversity. I have devoted chapters 1 to 4 in my earlier book to describing how a church can create these unity building events and ministries. If the reader seeks insight on this topic, please consult the above-mentioned book.

Chapter Eleven: Stage 6: Group Exit or Retention?

1. Henry David Thoreau, "A Week on the Concord and Merrimack Rivers," 1894.

2. Soon after Bill's departure, the denomination sent another pastor to the church. The church leaders had requested a pastor with more ambassadorial skills than Bill, and a very traditional pastor in his late sixties was hired. The new pastor called for a moratorium on change. However, the appointment of an aging pastor who appeared to be wary of change only further estranged the change proponents.

Two years later, the denomination closed the dwindling church. Third Church, which only a few years before was brimming with promise, was now disbanded; standing as a testimony to the powerful forces inherent in the change process.

What had happened? Why had denominational attempts to steady the course only further weakened the church's cohesiveness? "It's just the usual way things get handled in our denomination," stated one regional official. He was describing how traditional pastors are customarily sent to settle things down in churches that are undergoing conflict with newcomers. "The goal is to bring newcomers more in line with our way of thinking," he concluded. However, the appointment of this traditional and aging pastor had not eradicated the problem, only exacerbated it.

3. To those unfamiliar with church conflict, such emotional outbusts may seem implausible. But these are far from being the most impassioned outbursts that have taken place within congregations. The reason for such zealousness appears to be rooted in the importance of two connections found at church: connections with friends and connections with God.

Connections with friends: Congregants cherish the spiritual connection they receive from Christian fellowship. They do not want to see their friends estranged from the church and fellowship with them severed. As a result, any thought of adopting change that could alienate them or their friends releases a wave of passion.

Connections with God: Church attendees also value the spiritual connection they make with God during worship. As a rule, people generally worship most effortlessly in a familiar, comfortable environment. Changing elements of the worship liturgy and expression threaten to interrupt their spiritual connection with unfamiliarity and unpleasantness. Again, any thought of degrading their worship connections with unfamiliar or alien additions releases intense emotions.

4. I focused on the age orientation of church subgroups in *A House Divided: Bridging the Generation Gaps in Your Church*. In fact, in most churches, subgroups of change proponents as well as the status quo will develop around generations, with Boomers and Generation X gravitating toward change

proponents, and their elders showing a preference for the status quo. However, for the present discussion, age designations are not as important to grasp as the orientation toward change that each group embraces.

5. George C. Hunter, *The Contagious Congregation* (Nashville: Abingdon Press, 1979), 63.

6. Bob Whitesel and Kent R. Hunter, *A House Divided: Bridging the Generation Gaps in Your Church* (Nashville: Abingdon Press, 2000), 27-29.

7. Ibid., 187.

Chapter Twelve: Two Actions and an Attitude That Can Keep Your Change Proponents (and Your Status Quo Too!)

1. Henry Kissinger, *Wilson Library Bulletin*, March 1979.

2. For a step-by-step description of how to "trickle down" a viewpoint from the leadership team to the congregants, see Bob Whitesel and Kent R. Hunter, *A House Divided: Bridging the Generation Gaps in Your Church* (Nashville: Abingdon Press, 2000), 117-20. Especially helpful will be figure 5.3 on page 114, titled "The Trickle Down Effect."

3. C. Peter Wagner, *Apostles of the City* (Colorado Springs, Col.: Wagner Publications, 2000), 21.

4. Benjamin Franklin, Letter to J. B. LeRoy, November 12, 1789.

5. See Acts 15:36-41 for a fuller picture on how conflict can extend the reach of the good news. Though this is not the preferred pattern, on some occasions, group exit can actually be beneficial to a congregation. In chapter 3, "The Pain (and Gain) of Exits" I have tendered some illustrations of this atypical phenomena.